MASTERING ONCOLOGY EFFICACY ANALYSIS: ESSENTIAL SAS TECHNIQUES AND STATISTICAL METHODS

PRACTICAL APPLICATIONS FOR EFFICACY DATA AND TUMOR ASSESSMENT

SHIVA RAVINDRA

Made with ♥ on the Notion Press Platform
www.notionpress.com

To all the researchers, clinicians, and statistical programmers dedicated to advancing cancer treatment, and to the patients who inspire our work every day. Special thanks to SAS for empowering us with the tools to make a difference.

Shivravindra

Contents

Foreword

In the evolving landscape of clinical research, the role of statistical programming has become both foundational and transformative. This book offers a timely and practical guide into one of the most complex yet impactful areas—oncology programming and survival analysis.

Through detailed examples, clear explanations, and real-world SAS implementations, the content bridges the gap between statistical theory and hands-on application. It highlights the essential collaboration between statisticians and programmers, and emphasizes the depth of understanding required to navigate therapeutic guidelines, endpoint definitions, censoring rules, and regulatory expectations.

Whether you are an aspiring statistical programmer or an experienced professional looking to deepen your oncology knowledge, this book is structured to equip you with the tools to transform raw clinical data into meaningful, validated analysis outputs. More importantly, it empowers you to contribute confidently and efficiently within cross-functional clinical teams.

I commend the author for their clarity of vision and commitment to sharing knowledge that is not only technically sound, but also aligned with the real demands of today's clinical trial environment.

Preface

The motivation behind writing this book stems from a clear and growing need among statistical programmers working in oncology trials—to not only execute programs, but to truly understand the why behind each dataset, derivation, and analysis.

Throughout my career in clinical research, I've witnessed how the ability to interpret survival endpoints, apply censoring logic, and navigate domain-specific standards such as RECIST can empower programmers to contribute far more meaningfully to trial analysis and reporting. This book is intended to serve as a practical companion for both newcomers and experienced professionals, offering guidance rooted in real-world scenarios and best practices.

The chapters are structured to progressively build your understanding, from core survival analysis concepts and dataset specifications to advanced graphical reporting such as waterfall and forest plots. Emphasis has been placed on aligning programming logic with the Statistical Analysis Plan (SAP), helping bridge the gap between clinical objectives and analytical execution.

I hope this book not only enhances your technical skillset, but also strengthens your confidence to collaborate with statisticians, contribute to clinical decisions, and grow as a valuable member of the clinical trial team.

Thank you for allowing this book to be a part of your journey.

— [ShivaRavindra]

Clinical SAS Programmer | Oncology Specialist

Acknowledgements

This book would not have been possible without the support, encouragement, and guidance of many individuals who inspired me along the way.

First and foremost, I would like to express my sincere gratitude to my mentors and colleagues in the clinical research industry who challenged me to think deeper, code smarter, and understand the bigger picture behind every analysis. Your insights and feedback have been invaluable.

A special thanks to the statisticians I've had the privilege to work with—your collaborative spirit and willingness to share your expertise helped shape my understanding of survival analysis and oncology endpoints.

I am also deeply thankful to my family for their unwavering support and patience throughout this journey. Your belief in me has been my greatest motivation.

To my students, viewers, and followers in the SAS and clinical programming community—you have been a constant source of inspiration. Your curiosity, questions, and enthusiasm are the reason this book exists.

Lastly, I would like to thank every reader who picks up this book with the intention to grow, learn, and make a meaningful contribution to clinical research. I hope it serves you well.

Prologue

Clinical trials are more than numbers—they are a journey of science, hope, and precision. Behind every figure in a table or curve on a plot lies the story of a patient, a protocol, and a global effort to bring effective therapies to those in need. In oncology, where time and response matter profoundly, the accuracy and integrity of statistical programming play a critical role in every milestone of drug development.

This book was born from the intersection of curiosity and necessity. As a statistical programmer, I realized early on that understanding the clinical and statistical context behind our code can dramatically elevate the quality and impact of our work. Survival analysis, censoring logic, and endpoint derivations aren't just technical details—they are the foundation upon which life-changing decisions are made.

The chapters that follow are designed to not only teach programming techniques but also to build a deeper appreciation for the "why" behind them. Whether it's generating a waterfall plot or interpreting hazard ratios, every topic is tied back to real-world oncology trial needs and regulatory expectations.

This is more than a technical guide—it is an invitation to approach programming with clarity, purpose, and clinical awareness.

Shivravindra

CHAPTER ONE

Useful SAS techniques in Efficacy Analysis for Oncology studies

Cancer is characterized by abnormal and uncontrollable cell growth.

<u>Characteristics:</u>

§Invasion: Cancer cells can invade nearby tissues.

§Metastasis: Ability to spread to other parts of the body through the bloodstream or lymphatic system.

•Analyzing oncology studies is challenging due to the complex design and endpoints of studies within oncology.

•Statistical programmers generate oncology-related analysis data structures, produce meaningful tables, figures, and listings containing oncology-specific data based on statistical analysis plan (SAP) and specifications.

•However, this can be difficult for programmers who are unfamiliar with oncology-specific practices and guidelines.

• This book gives an introduction to oncology-specific studies, endpoints, and its unique statistical analysis techniques, in order to provide statistical programmers with the necessary background knowledge to work in oncology studies.

CHAPTER TWO

INTRODUCTION TO ONCOLOGY STUDIES

Studies in oncology and those in other therapeutic fields differ in many ways.

The following list summarizes some of the key differences that statistical programmers that are new to the field should understand.

I) Endpoints

In oncology studies, the most commonly used endpoints are

1)objective response rate (the proportion of responders, complete or partial, among all eligible subjects)

A phase-2 open label multi centre study of single agent ENZASTAURIN patients with Relapsed cutaneous T-cell Lymphoma

Primary Objective

To determine the Overall objective tumour responsive rate of the given drug in patient with the Relapsed cutaneous T-cell Lymphoma

The response rate is reported as the percentage of patients who achieve a complete response (CR) or partial response (PR) out of the total number of patients evaluated.

For example, if a treatment regimen achieves a response rate of 40%, it means that 40% of patients experienced either a complete or partial response to the treatment

2) overall survival (OS, time from randomization to death from any cause),

3) progression-free survival (PFS, time from randomization to disease progression or death)

A Randomized phase 3 study of MRTX949 versus Docetaxel in patients with previously treated Non-small cell lung cancer with KRAS G12C Mutation

Primary Objective

PFS

OS

4) quality of life (QOL) [1].

EQ-5D is a standardized tool used in healthcare to measure a patient's health-related quality of life (HRQoL) across different domains.

It provides a comprehensive assessment of a patient's well-being, including physical, mental, and social aspects.

EQ-5D descriptive system: This component assesses health status across five dimensions:

a. Mobility: the patient's ability to move around.

b. Self-care: the patient's ability to perform self-care activities.

c. Usual activities: the patient's ability to engage in daily activities, such as work, study, or household chores.

d. Pain/discomfort: the presence and severity of pain or discomfort.

e. Anxiety/depression: the presence and severity of anxiety or depression symptoms.

II) Data Collection

In addition to standard safety data, oncology trials require **more information to be collected in the CRFs** to evaluate the efficiency of the trials.

This information includes

- tumor measurements, their responses,
- ecog performance statuses.

ECOG Performance Status

External ID: ECOG

Design Object Name: ECOG

Short Label: ECOG Performance Status

Restricted: No

ECOG Performance Status		
Collection Date		External ID: QSDAT Required Future Date
Result	○ 0 - Fully active, able to carry on all pre-disease performance without restriction (0) ○ 1 - Restricted in physically strenuous activity but ambulatory and able to carry out work of a light or sedentary nature, e.g., light house work, office work (1) ○ 2 - Ambulatory and capable of all selfcare but unable to carry out any work activities; up and about more than 50% of waking hours (2)	External ID: ECOG101_QSORRES Required

CRF

Tumor Identification/Results Injected Lesions

External ID: TU

Design Object Name: TU

Short Label: Tumor Identification/Resu

Restricted: No

Tumor Identification/Results Injected Lesions		
Lesion Number	○ Injected Lesion #1 (INJ01) ○ Injected Lesion #2 (INJ02) ○ Injected Lesion #3 (INJ03)	External ID: TULNKID Required
Lesion location		External ID: TULOC Required Max Length: 100
Previously Irradiated	○ No (N)	External ID: PREIRRAD

CRF

III) Adverse Event Reporting

The National Cancer Institute (NCI) has developed oncology-specific guidelines for adverse event reporting, known as the National Terminology Criteria for Adverse Events (CTCAE).

In CTCAE, each AE is rated on a scale from 1 to 5, depending on severity (grade 1 corresponds to mild and grade 5 corresponds to death).

Every AE is also coded to preferred term and system organ class using the Medical Dictionary for Regulatory Activities (MedDRA) and additionally, classified by severity scales via CTCAE.

Common Terminology Criteria for Adverse Events (CTCAE)

Version 5.0

Published: November 27, 2017

U.S. DEPARTMENT OF HEALTH AND HUMAN SERVICES

National Institutes of Health

National Cancer Institute

CTCAE

Introduction
The NCI Common Terminology Criteria for Adverse Events is a descriptive terminology which can be utilized for Adverse Event (AE) reporting. A grading (severity) scale is provided for each AE term.

SOC
System Organ Class (SOC), the highest level of the MedDRA[1] hierarchy, is identified by anatomical or physiological system, etiology, or purpose (e.g., SOC Investigations for laboratory test results). CTCAE terms are grouped by MedDRA Primary SOCs. Within each SOC, AEs are listed and accompanied by descriptions of severity (Grade).

CTCAE Terms
An Adverse Event (AE) is any unfavorable and unintended sign (including an abnormal laboratory finding), symptom, or disease temporally associated with the use of a medical treatment or procedure that may or may not be considered related to the medical treatment or procedure. An AE is a term that is a unique representation of a specific event used for medical documentation and scientific analyses. Each CTCAE v4.0 term is a MedDRA LLT (Lowest Level Term).

Grades
Grade refers to the severity of the AE. The CTCAE displays Grades 1 through 5 with unique clinical descriptions of severity for each AE based on this general guideline:

Grade 1 Mild; asymptomatic or mild symptoms; clinical or diagnostic observations only; intervention not indicated.
Grade 2 Moderate; minimal, local or noninvasive intervention indicated; limiting age-appropriate instrumental ADL*.
Grade 3 Severe or medically significant but not immediately life-threatening; hospitalization or prolongation of hospitalization indicated; disabling; limiting self care ADL**.
Grade 4 Life-threatening consequences; urgent intervention indicated.
Grade 5 Death related to AE.

A Semi-colon indicates 'or' within the description of the grade.

A single dash (-) indicates a Grade is not available. Not all Grades are appropriate for all AEs. Therefore, some AEs are listed with fewer than five options for Grade selection.

Grade 5
Grade 5 (Death) is not appropriate for some AEs and therefore is not an option.

Definitions
A brief Definition is provided to clarify the meaning of each AE term. A single dash (-) indicates a Definition is not available.

Navigational Notes
A Navigational Note is used to assist the reporter in choosing a correct AE. It may list other AEs that should be considered in addition to or in place of the AE in question. A single dash (-) indicates a Navigational Note has not been defined for the AE term.

Activities of Daily Living (ADL)
*Instrumental ADL refer to preparing meals, shopping for groceries or clothes, using the telephone, managing money, etc.
**Self care ADL refer to bathing, dressing and undressing, feeding self, using the toilet, taking medications, and not bedridden.

Blood and lymphatic system disorders					
CTCAE Term	Grade 1	Grade 2	Grade 3	Grade 4	Grade 5
Anemia	Hemoglobin (Hgb) <LLN - 10.0 g/dL; <LLN - 6.2 mmol/L; <LLN - 100 g/L	Hgb <10.0 - 8.0 g/dL; <6.2 - 4.9 mmol/L; <100 - 80g/L	Hgb <8.0 g/dL; <4.9 mmol/L; <80 g/L; transfusion indicated	Life-threatening consequences; urgent intervention indicated	Death
Definition: A disorder characterized by a reduction in the amount of hemoglobin in 100 ml of blood. Signs and symptoms of anemia may include pallor of the skin and mucous membranes, shortness of breath, palpitations of the heart, soft systolic murmurs, lethargy, and fatigability. **Navigational Note:** -					
Bone marrow hypocellular	Mildly hypocellular or <=25% reduction from normal cellularity for age	Moderately hypocellular or >25 - <50% reduction from normal cellularity for age	Severely hypocellular or >50 - <=75% reduction cellularity from normal for age	Aplastic persistent for longer than 2 weeks	Death
Definition: A disorder characterized by the inability of the bone marrow to produce hematopoietic elements. **Navigational Note:** -					
Disseminated intravascular coagulation	-	Laboratory findings with no bleeding	Laboratory findings and bleeding	Life-threatening consequences; urgent intervention indicated	Death
Definition: A disorder characterized by systemic pathological activation of blood clotting mechanisms which results in clot formation throughout the body. There is an increase in the risk of hemorrhage as the body is depleted of platelets and coagulation factors. **Navigational Note:** -					
Eosinophilia	>ULN and >Baseline	-	Steroids initiated	-	-
Definition: A disorder characterized by laboratory test results that indicate an increased number of eosinophils in the blood. **Navigational Note:** -					
Febrile neutropenia	-	-	ANC <1000/mm3 with a single	Life-threatening	Death

For safety analysis, treatment-emergent adverse events (TEAEs) are commonly the main focus.

The treatment-emergent period is typically defined as the period of time from the **first dose date on a study drug to a pre-specified period of time (e.g. 28 days, 30 days) after the last dose date**.

In a crossover study (cross over from placebo to study drug), the derivation of treatment-emergent period can be more complex since it's needed to be carefully determined which treatment is the truly trigger for the AEs.

The incidence rates of TEAEs are typically summarized by system organ class (SOC) and preferred term (PT) in terms of severity, relationship to the drug, cause of dose reduction, etc

- ## Adverse Events

Treatment-emergent adverse events (TEAEs) are defined as signs or symptoms that emerge during treatment or within 28 days of the last dose of Investigational Product, including those signs and symptoms that have been absent pre-treatment or that have worsened relative to the pre-treatment assessment. Any adverse event considered related to treatment will also be considered a TEAE, regardless of the elapsed time since the last dose of Investigational Product.

project SAP

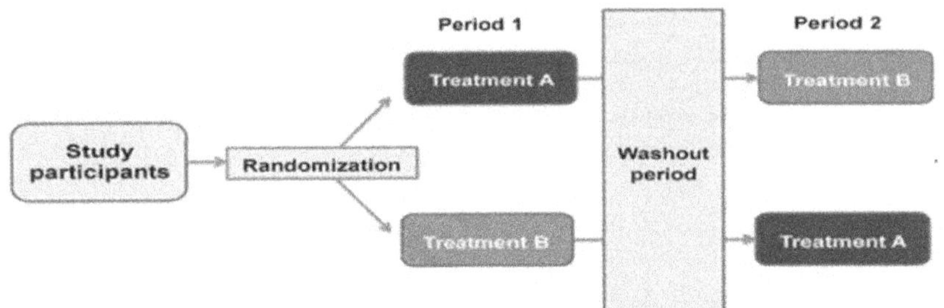

USUBJID Unique Subject Identifier	AEDECOD Dictionary Derived Term	TRTEMFL Treatment Emergent Analysis Flag	FUPFL Follow-up Flag	APERIOD Period	APHASE Phase	TRTA Actual Treatment
001	VOMITING	Y		1	FIRST TRT	A
001	HEADACHE	Y		2	SECOND TRT	B
001	ORAL HERPES		Y		FOLLOW-UP	

IV) Tumor measurement and assessment under RECIST guidelines

In oncology, **RECIST** is the primary tool used to access tumor progression or shrinkage for solid tumor.

RECIST (Response Evaluation Criteria In Solid Tumors):

•Standard system to measure how cancer responds to different treatments.

•Responses are provided based on change in tumor size using imaging.

•Radiologists identify Tumor and Non-Tumor based on RECIST pre-specified criteria

In RECIST [2], tumor lesions are first categorized as measurable or non-measurable at baseline.

Among the measurable lesions, **target lesions** are identified and recorded the baseline measurements.

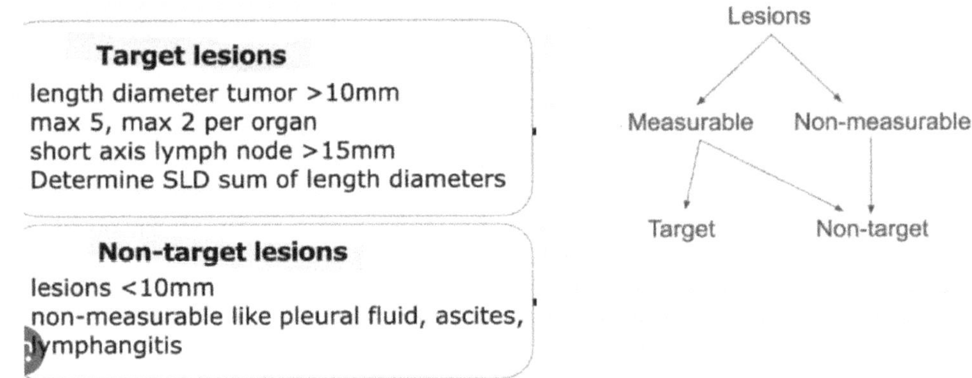

Measurable vs. Non-measurable Lesions

During treatment, subsequent measurements are performed for all target, non-target, and new lesions at each pre-specified time-point.

The changes in tumor size determine tumor response, and the response at each time point is evaluated as follows:

I) For target lesions

1) Complete Response (CR):

Disappearance of all target lesions.

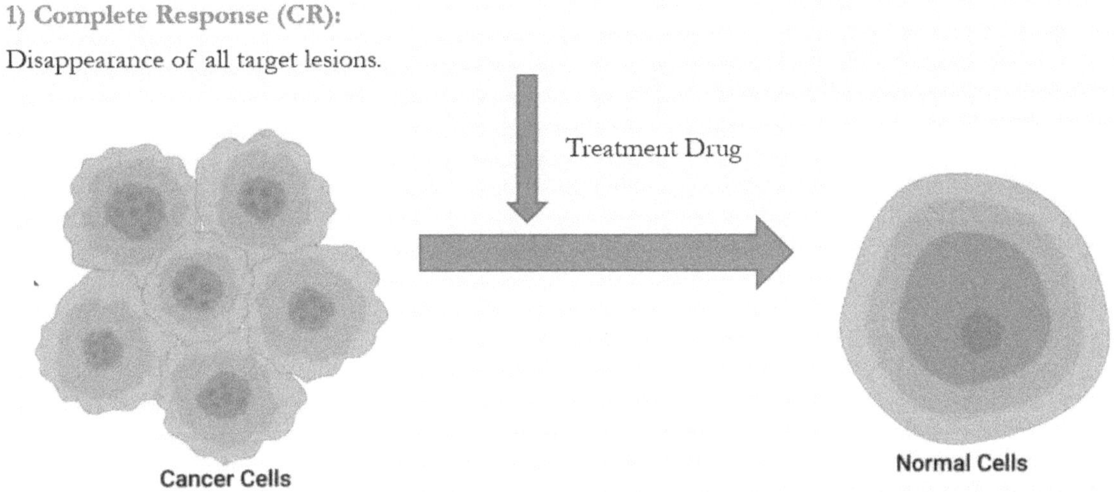

I) For target lesions

2) Partial Response (PR):

At least a **30% decrease** in the sum of diameters of target lesions, taking as reference the baseline sum diameters.

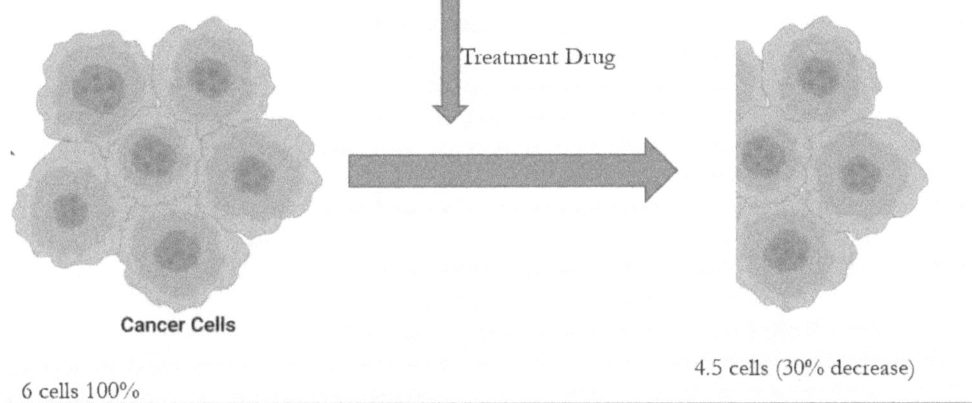

I) For target lesions

3)Progressive Disease (PD):

At least a **20% increase** in the sum of diameters of target lesions, taking as reference the smallest sum on study; or the appearance of one or more new lesions.

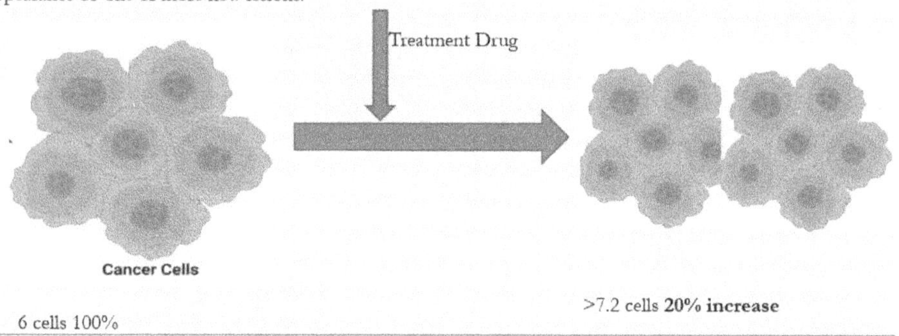

I) For target lesions

4) Stable Disease (SD):

Neither sufficient shrinkage to qualify for PR nor sufficient increase to qualify for PD.

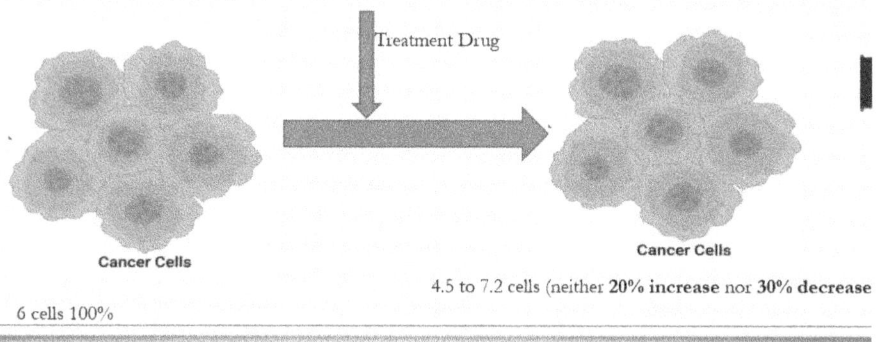

II) For non-target lesions

1) Complete Response (CR):

Disappearance of all non-target lesions and normalization of tumor marker level.

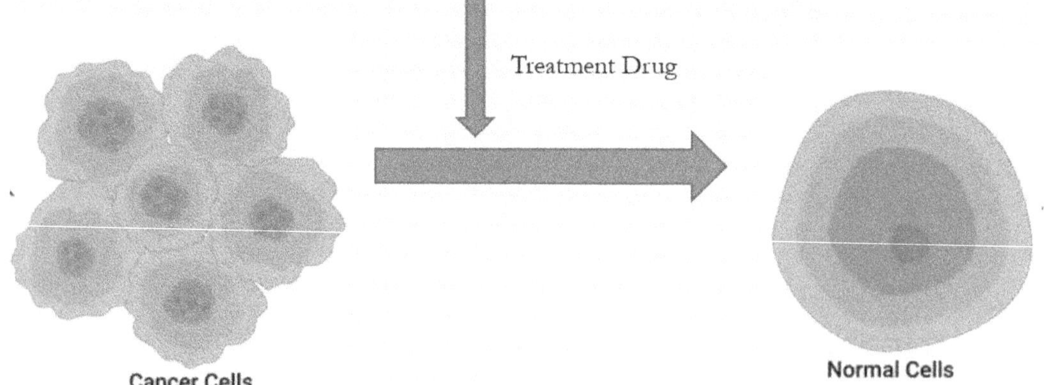

II) For non-target lesions

2) Non-CR/Non-PD

Persistence of one or more non-target lesion(s) and/or maintenance of **tumor marker level above the normal limits.**

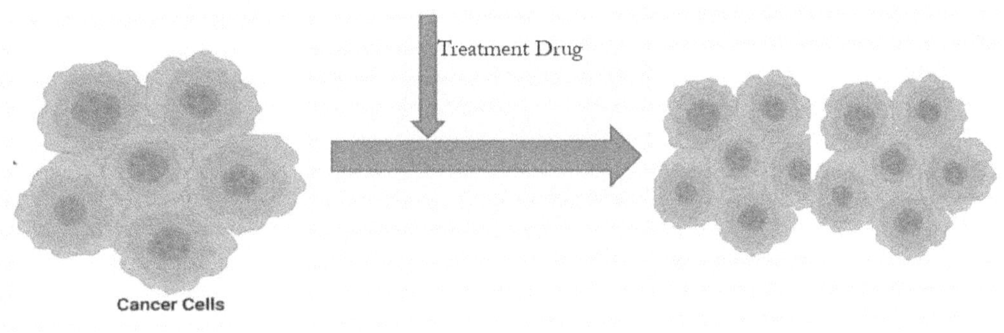

II) For non-target lesions

3) Progressive Disease (PD):

Unequivocal progression of existing non-target lesions or appearance of one or more new lesions.

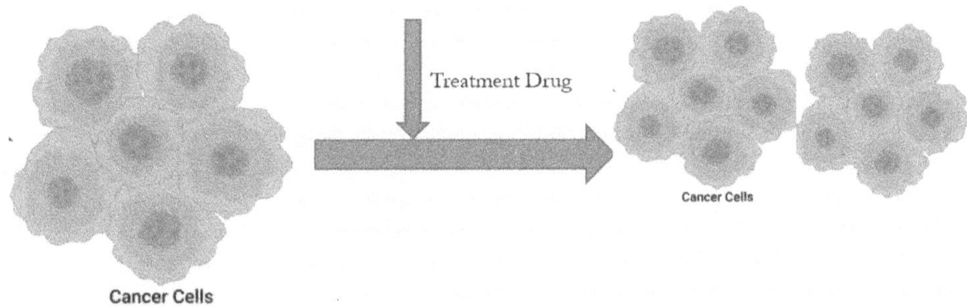

Per RECIST, the **best overall response** at the subject level is the **best response recorded** from the start of the treatment until disease progression, taking confirmation requirements into account.

```
invalue aval_resp
    "CR" = 1
    "PR" = 2
    "SD" = 3
    "NON-CR/NON-PD" = 4
    "NE" = 5
    "PD" = 6
    other = -1
```

V)Oncology specific SDTM domains

Here are some notes on TU (Tumor Identification), TR (Tumor Results), and RS (Response to Therapy) domains in the SDTM (Study Data Tabulation Model) specifically for oncology studies:

1. TU (Tumor Identification) Domain

Purpose: The TU domain captures information about the identification and characterization of tumors observed in a clinical trial. It includes the location, type, and method of detection for each tumor.

Key Variables:

TUSTRESC (Tumor Identification Result): Captures the qualitative result, like "Yes" or "No," indicating whether a tumor was identified.

TULOC (Location of Tumor): Specifies the anatomical location of the tumor (e.g., "Lung," "Liver").

TUMETHOD (Tumor Detection Method): Details the method used to detect the tumor, such as "CT Scan," "MRI," or "Physical Examination."

TUDTC (Date/Time of Tumor Identification): Records the date and time when the tumor was first identified.

2. TR (Tumor Results) Domain

Purpose: The TR domain captures the measurements and assessments of tumors over the course of the trial. This includes size, response to treatment, and progression status.

Key Variables:

TRTEST (Tumor Assessment Test Name): Describes the type of assessment or measurement performed, such as "Tumor Diameter."

TRORRES (Original Result): Records the original measurement or result, such as "3.5 cm" for a tumor size.

TRSTRESC (Standardized Result): Provides a standardized result, useful for comparisons across different sites or methods.

TRDY (Study Day of Tumor Assessment): Indicates the study day on which the tumor was assessed.

TRMETHOD (Method of Tumor Assessment): Similar to TUMETHOD, it specifies the method used to assess the tumor (e.g., "CT Scan," "MRI").

TRDTC (Date/Time of Tumor Assessment): The date and time when the tumor assessment was conducted.

3. RS (Response to Therapy) Domain

Purpose: The RS domain is used to record the response of tumors to the therapy being tested in the trial. This includes whether tumors are shrinking, stable, or growing, and whether new tumors have appeared.

Key Variables:

RSTEST (Response Test Name): Specifies the criteria or method used to assess the response (e.g., "RECIST 1.1," "WHO Criteria").

RSORRES (Original Result): The observed response result, such as "Partial Response," "Stable Disease," or "Progressive Disease."

RSSTRESC (Standardized Result): Provides a standardized version of the response result, allowing for comparison across different studies.

RSACPTFL (Accepted Response Flag): Indicates whether the response assessment is accepted according to protocol criteria.

RSDTC (Date/Time of Response Assessment): The date and time when the response assessment was performed.

4. Relationship Between TU, TR, and RS Domains

Sequential Use:

TU captures the initial identification of tumors in the study.

TR tracks ongoing measurements and assessments of these tumors during the study.

RS evaluates the tumors' response to the therapy, summarizing the effectiveness of the treatment.

Linkage: These domains are linked by unique identifiers, such as subject ID and tumor ID, allowing for integrated analysis of how tumors respond to treatment over time.

Importance in Oncology Trials: These domains are crucial for regulatory submissions as they provide a structured way to document and analyze tumor-related data, helping to demonstrate the efficacy of oncology therapies.

5. Standardization and Compliance

SDTM Compliance: Using these domains ensures that the trial data are compliant with SDTM standards, which is required by regulatory bodies like the FDA and EMA for submissions.

Data Consistency: Standardization across trials enables consistent and comparable reporting of tumor data, which is essential for meta-analyses and cross-study comparisons.

These notes should provide a clear understanding of the TU, TR, and RS domains in the context of oncology trials within the SDTM framework.

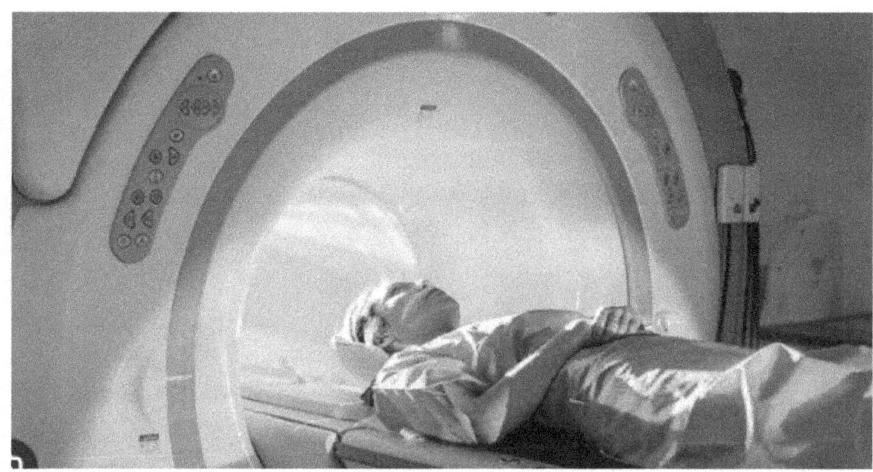

Magnetic resonance imaging (MRI) is a test that can be used to find a tumor in the body and to help find out whether a tumor is cancerous. Doctors also use it to learn more about cancer after they find it, including: The size and location of the tumor. To plan cancer treatments, such as surgery or radiation therapy.

MRI
CT
X-RAY

TU

Target lesions

length diameter tumor >10mm
max 5, max 2 per organ
short axis lymph node >15mm
Determine SLD sum of length diameters

Non-target lesions

lesions <10mm
non-measurable like pleural fluid, ascites,
lymphangitis

Lesions are abnormal changes in an organ or
in tissue due to injury or disease.

TU

IDENTIFY TUMORS

TULNKID	TUTESTCD	TUTEST	TUORRES
NT01	TUMIDENT	Tumor Identification	NON-TARGET
NT02	TUMIDENT	Tumor Identification	NON-TARGET
NT03	TUMIDENT	Tumor Identification	NON-TARGET
NT04	TUMIDENT	Tumor Identification	NON-TARGET
NT05	TUMIDENT	Tumor Identification	NON-TARGET
NT06	TUMIDENT	Tumor Identification	NON-TARGET
NT07	TUMIDENT	Tumor Identification	NON-TARGET
NT08	TUMIDENT	Tumor Identification	NON-TARGET
NT09	TUMIDENT	Tumor Identification	NON-TARGET
NT10	TUMIDENT	Tumor Identification	NON-TARGET
T01	TUMIDENT	Tumor Identification	TARGET
T02	TUMIDENT	Tumor Identification	TARGET
T03	TUMIDENT	Tumor Identification	TARGET
NT01	TUMIDENT	Tumor Identification	NON-TARGET
NT02	TUMIDENT	Tumor Identification	NON-TARGET
NT03	TUMIDENT	Tumor Identification	NON-TARGET
NT04	TUMIDENT	Tumor Identification	NON-TARGET
NT05	TUMIDENT	Tumor Identification	NON-TARGET
NT06	TUMIDENT	Tumor Identification	NON-TARGET
NT07	TUMIDENT	Tumor Identification	NON-TARGET
NT08	TUMIDENT	Tumor Identification	NON-TARGET
NT09	TUMIDENT	Tumor Identification	NON-TARGET
NT10	TUMIDENT	Tumor Identification	NON-TARGET

TU

TULOC	TUMETHOD
SMALL BREAST MASS AND INFEROLATERAL ASPECT OF LEFT BREAST	CONTRAST ENHANCED CT SCAN
ENHANCING LESIONS IN THE MEDIAL ASPECT OF THE LEFT BREAST	CONTRAST ENHANCED CT SCAN
LEFT RIB CAGE/FLANK SUBCUTANEOUS #1	CLINICAL EVALUATION
LEFT RIB CAGE/FLANK SUBCUTANEOUS #3	CLINICAL EVALUATION
LEFT RIB CAGE/FLANK SUBCUTANEOUS #5	CLINICAL EVALUATION
LEFT RIB CAGE/FLANK SUBCUTANEOUS #6	CLINICAL EVALUATION
LEFT RIB CAGE/SUBCUTANEOUS #7	CLINICAL EVALUATION
LEFT RIB CAGE/SUBCUTANEOUS #8	CLINICAL EVALUATION
LEFT RIB CAGE/SUBCUTANEOUS #9	CLINICAL EVALUATION
LEFT RIB CAGE/FLANK SUBCUTANEOUS #10 (IL #3)	CLINICAL EVALUATION
MASS WITHIN INFERIOR LATERAL LEFT BREAST	CONTRAST ENHANCED CT SCAN
LEFT RIB CAGE/FLANK SUBCUTANEOUS #2 (IL #1)	CLINICAL EVALUATION
LEFT RIB CAGE/FLANK SUBCUTANEOUS #4 (IL #2)	CLINICAL EVALUATION
SMALL BREAST MASS AND INFEROLATERAL ASPECT OF LEFT BREAST	CONTRAST ENHANCED CT SCAN
ENHANCING LESIONS IN THE MEDIAL ASPECT OF THE LEFT BREAST	CONTRAST ENHANCED CT SCAN
LEFT RIB CAGE/FLANK SUBCUTANEOUS #1	CLINICAL EVALUATION
LEFT RIB CAGE/FLANK SUBCUTANEOUS #3	CLINICAL EVALUATION
LEFT RIB CAGE/FLANK SUBCUTANEOUS #5	CLINICAL EVALUATION
LEFT RIB CAGE/FLANK SUBCUTANEOUS #6	CLINICAL EVALUATION
LEFT RIB CAGE/SUBCUTANEOUS #7	CLINICAL EVALUATION
LEFT RIB CAGE/SUBCUTANEOUS #8	CLINICAL EVALUATION
LEFT RIB CAGE/SUBCUTANEOUS #9	CLINICAL EVALUATION

TU

MEASURE TUMORS
TR

TRGRPID	TRLNKID	TRTESTCD	TRTEST	TRORRES	TRORRESU
TARGET	T01	LDIAM	Longest Diameter	5	mm
TARGET	T02	LDIAM	Longest Diameter	12	mm
TARGET	T03	LDIAM	Longest Diameter	12	mm
TARGET	T04	LDIAM	Longest Diameter		
TARGET	T05	LDIAM	Longest Diameter		
TARGET		SUMLDIAM	Sum of Longest Diameter	29	mm
NON TARGET	NT01	TUMSTATE	Tumor State	PRESENT	

TR

MEASURE TUMORS

TRGRPID	TRLNKID	TRTESTCD	TRTEST	TRORRES
7 TARGET		SUMLDIAM	Sum of Longest Diameter	29
3 NON-TARGET	NT01	TUMSTATE	Tumor State	PRESENT
3 NON-TARGET	NT02	TUMSTATE	Tumor State	PRESENT
) NON-TARGET	NT03	TUMSTATE	Tumor State	PRESENT
1 NON-TARGET	NT04	TUMSTATE	Tumor State	PRESENT
2 NON-TARGET	NT05	TUMSTATE	Tumor State	PRESENT
3 NON-TARGET	NT06	TUMSTATE	Tumor State	PRESENT
4 NON-TARGET	NT07	TUMSTATE	Tumor State	PRESENT
5 NON-TARGET	NT08	TUMSTATE	Tumor State	PRESENT
5 NON-TARGET	NT09	TUMSTATE	Tumor State	PRESENT
7 NON-TARGET	NT10	TUMSTATE	Tumor State	PRESENT
3 TARGET	T01	LDIAM	Longest Diameter	NON EVALUABLE
1 TARGET	T02	LDIAM	Longest Diameter	12
NON-TARGET	NT01	TUMSTATE	Tumor State	PRESENT
NON-TARGET	NT02	TUMSTATE	Tumor State	UNABLE TO EVALUATE
NON-TARGET	NT03	TUMSTATE	Tumor State	UNABLE TO EVALUATE
NON-TARGET	NT04	TUMSTATE	Tumor State	UNABLE TO EVALUATE
NON-TARGET	NT05	TUMSTATE	Tumor State	UNABLE TO EVALUATE
NON-TARGET	NT06	TUMSTATE	Tumor State	UNABLE TO EVALUATE
NON-TARGET	NT07	TUMSTATE	Tumor State	UNABLE TO EVALUATE
NON-TARGET	NT08	TUMSTATE	Tumor State	UNABLE TO EVALUATE
TARGET	T01	LDIAM	Longest Diameter	22

TR

ACCESS RESPONSE RS

USUBJID	RSSEQ	RSGRPID	RSTESTCD	RSTEST	RSCAT	RSORRES	RSSTRESC
MMSC 2023-01-101001	5	NON-TARGET	OVRLNTR	Overall Non-target Response		Not Evaluated	NE
MMSC 2023-01-101001	7	TARGET	OVRLTRG	Overall Target Response		Not Evaluated	NE
MMSC 2023-01-101002	4	NON-TARGET	OVRLNTR	Overall Non-target Response		Not Evaluated	NE
MMSC 2023-01-101002	6	TARGET	OVRLTRG	Overall Target Response		Not Evaluated	NE
MMSC 2023-01-101003	5	NON-TARGET	OVRLNTR	Overall Non-target Response		Non-Complete Response/Non-Progressive Disease	SD
MMSC 2023-01-101003	7	TARGET	OVRLTRG	Overall Target Response		Stable Disease	SD
MMSC 2023-01-101006	2	NON-TARGET	OVRLNTR	Overall Non-target Response		Non-Complete Response/Non-Progressive Disease	SD
MMSC 2023-01-101006	4	TARGET	OVRLTRG	Overall Target Response		Stable Disease	SD
MMSC 2023-01-101007	5	NON-TARGET	OVRLNTR	Overall Non-target Response		Progressive Disease	PD
MMSC 2023-01-101007	7	TARGET	OVRLTRG	Overall Target Response		Stable Disease	SD

RS

VI. Censoring and confirmation rules

In oncology, *censoring* refers to the **situation where the exact outcome of interest** (such as **time to disease progression** or **survival time**) is not observed for some patients within the study period.

This could happen for various reasons, like when a patient leaves the study early, is lost to follow-up, or the study ends before they experience the event (e.g., death or relapse).

Example:

In a clinical trial for a new cancer drug, if a patient is still alive at the end of the study period, their survival time is *censored* because we don't know how much longer they will live after the study ends.

Thus, their exact survival time is unknown.

Censoring occurs when patients **haven't experience** any event of interest, or have not had a follow-up.

Most time-to-event endpoints require carefully reviewing the censoring rules and criteria for confirmation of progression.

For example, one of the most commonly used censoring rules for OS and PFS can be summarized as follows:

Table 1 is a summary of censoring rules.

Endpoint	Date of Event	Date of Censoring
OS	death date	date of last known alive
PFS	date of progression	date of last assessment/scan

Table 1 *Censoring Rules for OS and PFS as endpoints*

•In time-to-event ADaM dataset, the information of event or censoring is captured by the variable **CNSR**, with CNSR = 0 for events

CNSR > 0 for censored records.

Additionally, **date of event/censoring** is collected in **ADT** variable, associated with **AVAL variable** computing the **time to event/censoring from the origin**.

The general formula to calculate AVAL is typically

(ADT [Date of Event/Censoring] - randomization date + 1).

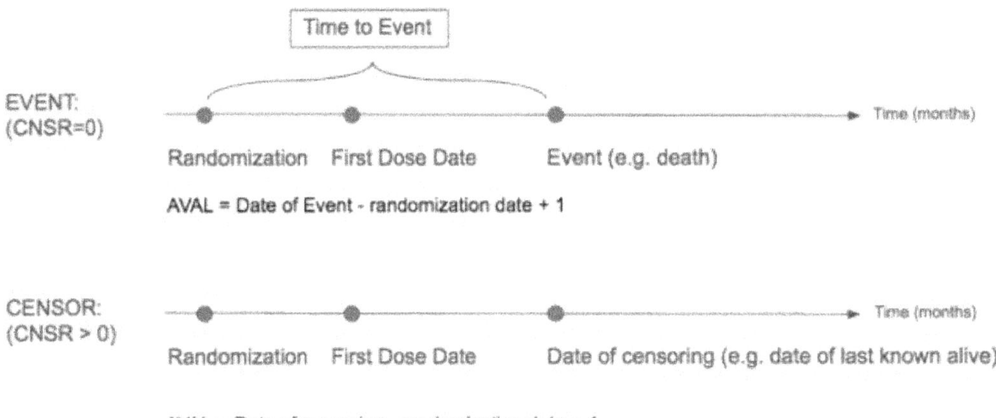

Table 2 is an example of ADTTE dataset, where OS is the event of interest.

SUBJID	PARAM	PARAMCD	RANDDT	ADT	AVAL	CNSR	EVNTDESC	EVNDTDSC
101	Time to Overall Survival	OS	2018-02-06	2018-12-02	9.85	0	Dead	Date of Death
102	Time to Overall Survival	OS	2018-02-11	2018-08-26	6.47	1	Alive	Date of Last Known Alive
103	Time to Overall Survival	OS	2018-02-13	2018-09-23	7.32	1	Lost to Follow-up	Date of Last Known Alive
104	Time to Overall Survival	OS	2018-02-22	2018-12-21	9.95	1	Dead after Analysis Cutoff	Analysis Cutoff Date

Table 2 An Example of ADTTE Dataset

Note that AVAL is calculated by analysis date in month: (ADT-RANDDT+1)/30.4375

USUBJID	PARAMCD	PARAM	CNSR	STARTDT	ADT	AVAL	EVNTDESC	CNSDTDSC
STDY101-102-01101	PFS	Progression Free Survival (Days)	0	2018-02-10	2018-04-10	60	DOCUMENTED PROGRESSION	
STDY101-102-01102	PFS	Progression Free Survival (Days)	0	2018-02-10	2018-07-02	143	DEATH	
STDY101-102-01103	PFS	Progression Free Survival (Days)	1	2018-02-10	2018-06-06	117	COMPLETED STUDY	LAST RADIOLOGIC ASSESSMENT SHOWING NO PROGRESSION
STDY101-102-01104	PFS	Progression Free Survival (Days)	1	2018-02-10	2018-02-10	1	NO BASELINE ASSESSMENT	RANDOMIZATION
STDY101-102-01105	PFS	Progression Free Survival (Days)	1	2018-02-10	2018-06-06	117	NEW ANTI-CANCER THERAPY	LAST RADIOLOGIC ASSESSMENT PRIOR TO NEW ANTI-CANCER THERAPY

VIII) Special statistical analysis for efficacy

Oncology trials involve special statistical techniques to analyze their efficacy.

Some of these techniques include

1) log-rank test to compare the OS/PFS between two treatment groups

The log-rank test is commonly used in survival analysis to compare the overall survival (OS) or progression-free survival (PFS) between two treatment groups.

In SAS, you can perform the log-rank test using the **PROC LIFETEST** procedure.

Below is an example to illustrate this.

time	status	treatment
5	1	1
8	0	1
10	1	1
12	1	2
15	0	2
18	1	2
20	0	1
22	1	2

```
proc lifetest data=survival_data plots=survival;
    time time*status(0);
    strata treatment;
run;
```

time: The time to event (either OS or PFS).
status: The event indicator (0 = censored, 1 = event occurred).
treatment: The treatment group (1 = Treatment A, 2 = Treatment B).

time time*status(0); specifies the time-to-event variable (time) and the censoring information (status), where 0 indicates censoring.
strata treatment; specifies that the log-rank test should compare the survival distributions between the levels of the treatment variable.
Plots=Survival: This option generates survival plots for visual comparison of the survival curves

```
ods graphics / reset imagename='SurvivalPlot' imagefmt=png;
ods listing gpath='G:\My Journey Drive\YT ONCOLOGY DEPTH\Day-7-05SEP2024';

proc lifetest data=survival_data plots=survival;
    time time*status(0);
    strata treatment;
run;

ods graphics off;
```

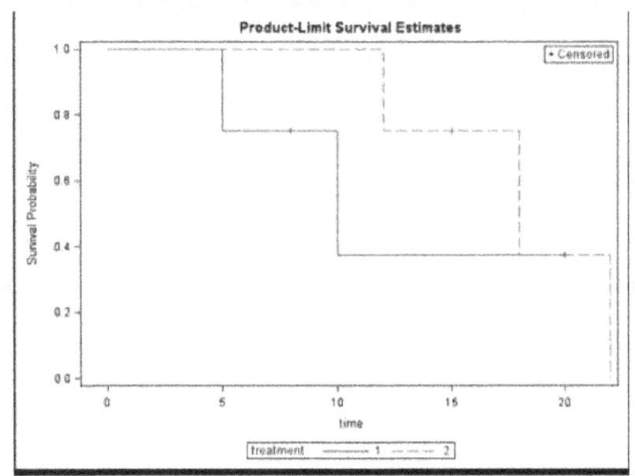


```
ods graphics / reset imagename='SurvivalPlot' imagefmt=png;
ods listing gpath='G:\My Journey Drive\YT ONCOLOGY DEPTH\Day-7-05SEP2024';

proc lifetest data=survival_data plots=survival;
    time time*status(1);
    strata treatment;
run;

ods graphics off;
```

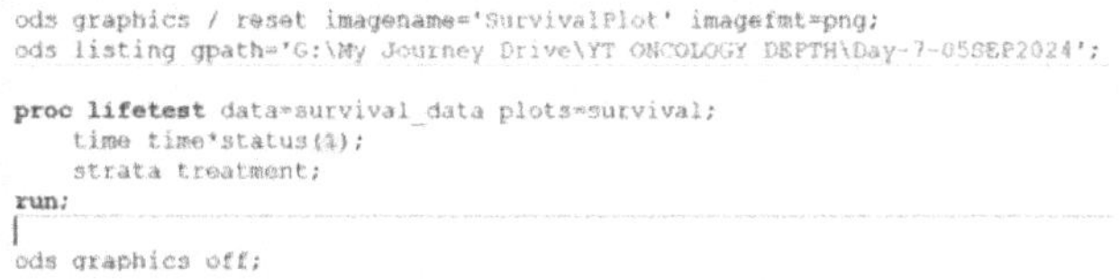

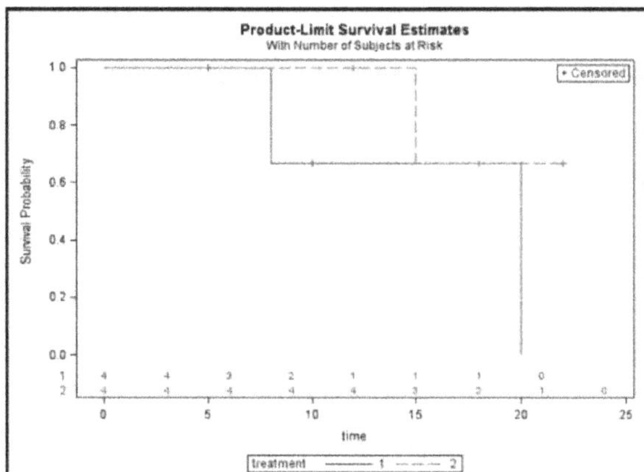

time time*status(1); treats a status of 1 as the event of interest, while all other statuses are treated as censored data.

time time*status(0); treats a status of 0 as the event of interest, while all other statuses are treated as censored data.

```
          Test of Equality over Strata

                                        Pr >
    Test       Chi-Square    DF     Chi-Square

    Log-Rank     0.4348       1       0.5096
    Wilcoxon     0.3289       1       0.5663
    -2Log(LR)    0.1120       1       0.7378
```

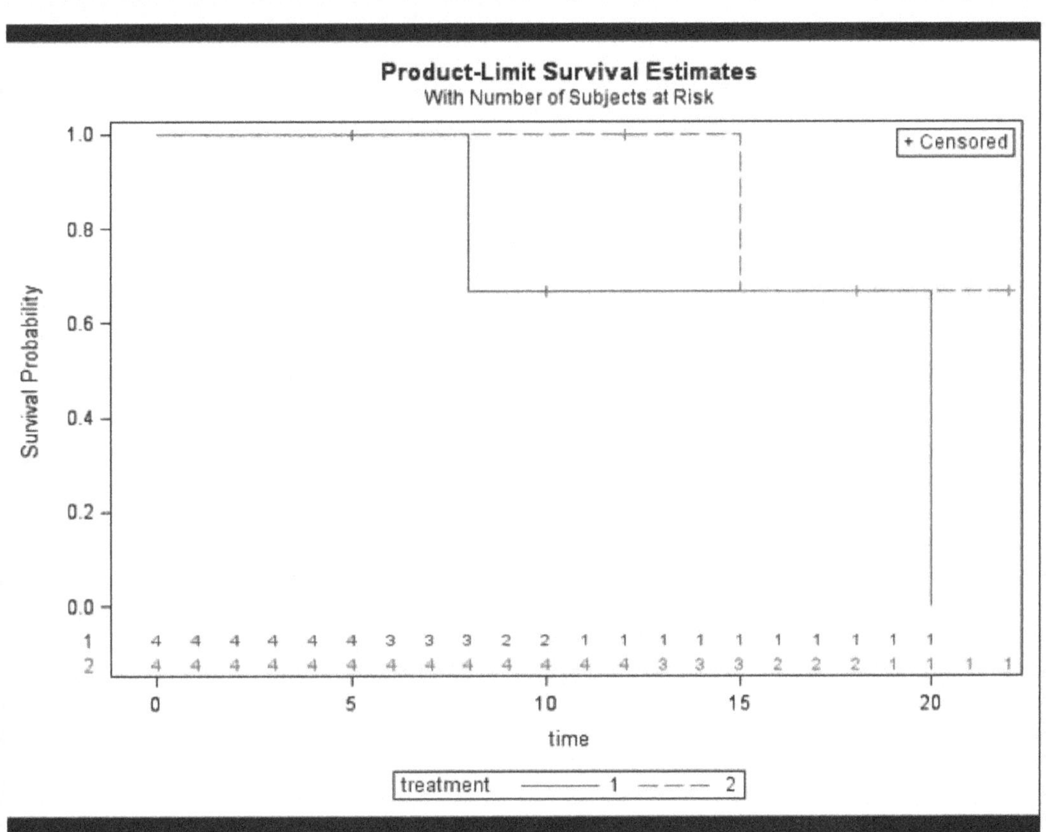

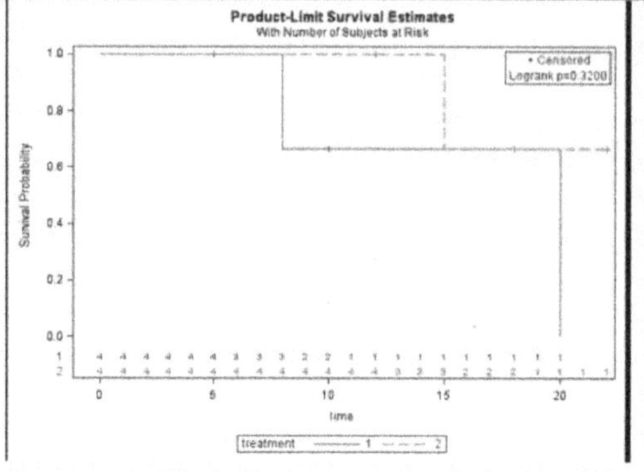

By adding the **test** option, you make it easier to interpret the plot, as it directly shows whether the differences in survival between the treatment groups are statistically significant.

```
ods graphics / reset imagename='SurvivalPlot' imagefmt=png;
ods listing gpath='G:\My Journey Drive\YT ONCOLOGY DEPTH\Day-7-05SEP2024';

proc lifetest data=survival_data plots=survival (atrisk=0 to 25 by 1 TEST);
    time time*status(1);
    strata treatment;
run;

ods graphics off;
```

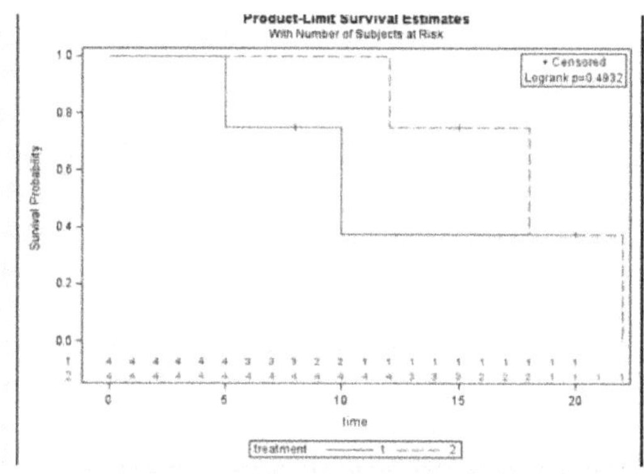

```
ods graphics / reset imagename='SurvivalPlot' imagefmt=png;
ods listing gpath='G:\My Journey Drive\YT ONCOLOGY DEPTH\Day-7-05SEP2024';

proc lifetest data=survival_data plots=survival (atrisk=0 to 25 by 1 TEST);
    time time*status(0);
    strata treatment;
run;

ods graphics off;
```

2) Kaplan-Meier curve

is an intuitive graphical representation of the **survival distribution** in different treatment groups.
In addition, **50th percentile of KM estimates** can be used as the estimate of the
median duration (time when half of the patients are event free) for time-to-event endpoints

The Kaplan-Meier curve is a fundamental tool in survival analysis that provides a visual representation of the probability of surviving or remaining event-free over time.

This is particularly useful in medical research, where the event could be death, relapse, or another significant occurrence

patient_id	group	time	status
1	A	5	1
2	A	8	1
3	A	12	0
4	A	15	1
5	B	7	1
6	B	9	1
7	B	13	0
8	B	16	1
9	B	10	1
10	B	14	0

```
ods graphics / reset imagename='SurvivalPlotS' imagefmt=png;
ods listing gpath='G:\My Journey Drive\YT ONCOLOGY DEPTH\Day-7-05SEP2024';

proc lifetest data=survival_data2 plots=survival;
    time time*status(0);
    strata group;
run;
ods graphics off;
```

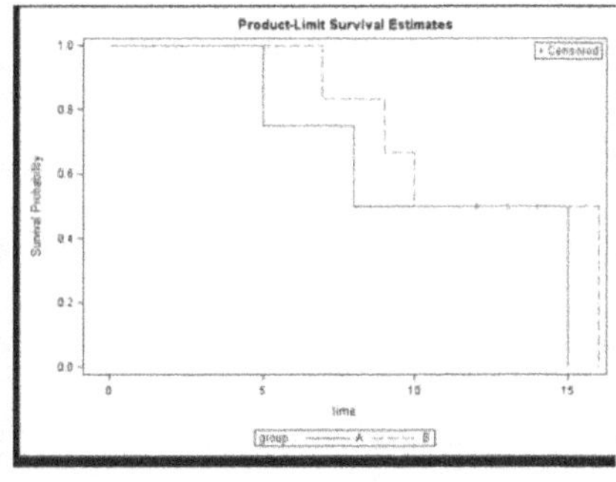


```
         Summary Statistics for Time Variable time

                    Quartile Estimates

                  Point          95% Confidence Interval
         Percent  Estimate  Transform   [Lower      Upper )

              75   16.0000   LOGLOG      9.0000     16.0000
              50   13.0000   LOGLOG      7.0000     16.0000
              25    9.0000   LOGLOG      7.0000     16.0000
```

The **log-rank test** and **Kaplan-Meier survival analysis** are both commonly used in survival analysis

Log-Rank Test	Kaplan-Meier Survival Analysis
Purpose: The log-rank test is a hypothesis test to compare the survival distributions of two or more groups.	**Purpose**: The Kaplan-Meier estimator is a non-parametric statistic used to estimate the survival function from lifetime data.
Output: It provides a p-value to test the null hypothesis that there is no difference in survival between the groups being compared.	**Output**: It produces a survival curve, which shows the probability of surviving over time for a cohort of subjects. The x-axis represents time, and the y-axis represents the survival probability.
Interpretation: If the p-value is below a certain threshold (commonly 0.05), the null hypothesis is rejected, indicating that there is a statistically significant difference in survival between the groups. The log-rank test complements the Kaplan-Meier survival curves by providing a formal statistical test for comparison	**Interpretation**: The curve helps visualize the fraction of subjects surviving for a certain period after treatment or diagnosis. It is useful for estimating the survival function and can be used to compare different groups (e.g., treated vs. untreated) visually.

3) The Reserve Kaplan-Meier (KM) method

is used in survival analysis to estimate **median follow-up time** by treating
loss-to-follow-up as events, and
the actual events of interest (like death or disease occurrence) as censored.

This approach can provide a more conservative estimate of follow-up time when there are significant amounts of loss-to-follow-up.

Concept:
Events: These are the actual outcomes of interest (e.g., death, disease recurrence).
Censoring: This usually refers to individuals who are lost to follow-up or who have not experienced the event by the end of the study.

In Reserve Kaplan-Meier, you reverse the usual roles:
Loss-to-follow-up is treated as an "event."
The actual events are treated as "censored."

```
/* Reverse events and censoring */
data reversed;
    set survival;
    if status = 1 then status = 0;   /* Treat events as censored */
    else if status = 0 then status = 1; /* Treat censored as events */
run;
ods graphics / reset imagename='SurvivalPloPP' imagefmt=png;
ods listing gpath='G:\My Journey Drive\YT ONCOLOGY DEPTH\Day-7-05SEP2024';

/* Kaplan-Meier Estimate */
proc lifetest data=reversed outsurv=km_estimate;
    time time*status(0);
run;
ods graphics off;
```

This approach helps in getting a more conservative **estimate of median follow-up time** by treating losses to follow-up as if they were events, thereby potentially reflecting a more cautious view of the follow-up period.

4) Cox regression provides us a way to **estimate** and **compare** the **survival experiences** of two treatment groups.

We typically calculate **Hazard ratio associated with Cox regression**, which refers to the **relevant risk of experiencing an event of interest** between two groups.

time	event	group
6	1	1
8	1	1
10	0	1
12	1	1
14	0	1
7	1	2
9	1	2
11	0	2
13	1	2
15	0	2

Example Scenario:
Suppose we have data on two groups of patients undergoing different treatments for cancer. We want to compare the survival experiences between these two groups.
Data:
Group 1: Treatment A
Group 2: Treatment B
Event: Death (1 if the patient died, 0 if the patient is still alive)
Time: Time in months from the start of the treatment until death or the end of the study.

Explanation:
•**time:** Time until the event (death) or end of study.
•**event:** Whether the event (death) occurred (1 = Yes, 0 = No).
•**group:** Treatment group (1 = Treatment A, 2 = Treatment B).

```
proc phreg data=survival_data;
   class group (ref='1'); /* Referenc
   model time*event(0) = group;
   hazardratio group;
run;
```

Explanation of the Code:

proc phreg: This procedure is used to fit the Cox proportional ha

class group (ref='1'); Specifies that the group variable is categori reference category.

model time*event(0) = group;

Models the time to event (death), with the event variable coded as The group variable is the predictor.

hazardratio group; Requests the calculation of the hazard ratio fo

```
                              The SAS System     00:00 Wednesday, September 3, 2014   4

                              The PHREG Procedure

                     Analysis of Maximum Likelihood Estimates

                       Parameter     Standard                                 Hazard
   Parameter   DF      Estimate        Error     Chi-Square    Pr > ChiSq      Ratio    Label

   group    2    1     -0.19935       0.82271       0.0587       0.8085        0.819    group 2

                            Hazard Ratios for group

                                 Point      95% Wald Confidence
                   Description   Estimate         Limits

                   group 1 vs 2    1.221      0.243      6.122
```

Output Interpretation:
Hazard Ratio (HR): If the HR for group is 1.221, this means that patients in Treatment B have 1.221 times the risk of dying compared to patients in Treatment A

5)Binomial test of binary proportion along with its confidence interval (Exact CI or normal approximation) to compare the **proportion of subjects free of event or the difference in response rates** at given landmark time points

group	event_free	total
A	35	50
B	40	50

Data:
Group 1: Treatment A (50 patients)
Group 2: Treatment B (50 patients)
Event-Free at 12 Months:
Treatment A: 35 out of 50 patients are event-free.
Treatment B: 40 out of 50 patients are event-free.

Exact Binomial Test with Confidence Interval:

```
proc freq data=event_data;
   tables group / binomial(EXACT) alpha=0.05;
   weight total;
   exact binomial;
run;
```

Explanation of the Code:
proc freq: This procedure is used to perform the Binomial test.
tables group / binomial(EXACT) alpha=0.05;
Specifies that we want to perform a binomial test on the group variable. The **alpha=0.05 option sets the confidence level at 95%.**
weight total;
We use the total variable as the weight to indicate the **number of patients** in each group.
exact binomial;
Requests the exact Binomial test and the exact confidence interval for the proportion.

Output Interpretation:
•**Proportion:** The proportion of event-free patients at 12 months in each group.
•**Confidence Interval (CI):** The 95% confidence interval for the proportion of event-free patients in each group.
•**P-Value:** The p-value from the binomial test tells us if the proportion of event-free patients is significantly different from a hypothesized value (e.g., comparing to 50%).

```
          The SAS System      00:00 Wednesday, September 3, 201-

              The FREQ Procedure

              Binomial Proportion
                  group = A

         Proportion (P)            0.5000
         ASE                       0.0500

    Confidence Limits for the Binomial Proportion
               Proportion = 0.5000

   Type                       95% Confidence Limits

   Clopper-Pearson (Exact)    0.3983          0.6017

      Type                    95% Confidence Limits

      Clopper-Pearson (Exact)   0.3983      0.6017

           Test of H0: Proportion = 0.5

         ASE under H0           0.0500
         Z                      0.0000
         One-sided Pr <  Z      0.5000
         Two-sided Pr >  |Z|    1.0000

             Sample Size = 100
```

Output Interpretation:
•**Proportion:** The observed proportion of event-free patients in each group.
•**Confidence Interval (CI):** The 95% confidence interval for the proportion.
•**P-Value:** Tests whether the proportion of event-free patients differs significantly from a specified proportion (e.g., 50%).

USEFUL SAS TECHNIQUES IN ONCOLOGY STUDIES

Efficacy time-to-event endpoints such as overall survival (OS), PFS (progression-free survival), and time to PSA (Prostate-specific Antigen) progression are typically evaluated by survival analysis.

Survival analysis takes into account the **censoring observations** (e.g. lost to follow up or no event occurs) and the
survival time refers to the time from starting point (e.g. randomization) to the occurrence of an event of interest (e.g. death).

There are three major SAS procedures for survival analysis [

PROC LIFETEST
PROC PHREG
PROC LIFEREG

1}**The PROC LIFETEST** procedure in SAS is commonly used to analyze survival data, and it provides both life tables and Kaplan-Meier (KM) survival estimates.
The KM estimate is a **non-parametric method** to estimate the survival function without assuming anything about the underlying hazard function or that hazards are proportional across groups.

A **non-parametric method** is a type of statistical method that does not assume a specific form or distribution for the underlying data (like normal distribution).

time	censor	group
5	1	A
8	1	A
10	0	A
12	1	A
4	1	B
7	1	B
9	0	B
11	1	B

```
* Run PROC LIFETEST to get Kaplan-Meier estimates;
proc lifetest data=survival_data plots=(s);
    time time*censor(0);   /* time is the event time, censor is the censoring varial
    strata group;          /* Compare KM curves between two groups (A and B) */
run;
```

Explanation of the Code:
DATA Step: We create a dataset called survival_data with three columns:
time: The time-to-event (survival time).
censor: This is the censoring variable where 1 indicates the event (death) occurred, and 0 indicates the event did not occur (censored).
group: This column has groups "A" and "B" to differentiate between two populations.

PROC LIFETEST: This procedure is used to generate Kaplan-Meier estimates.

time time*censor(0): The first time is the variable for time-to-event.
The second part censor(0) specifies the censoring variable and that 0 indicates a censored observation.
strata group: This compares the Kaplan-Meier curves between groups A and B.
plots=(s): This option generates the survival plot (Kaplan-Meier plot).

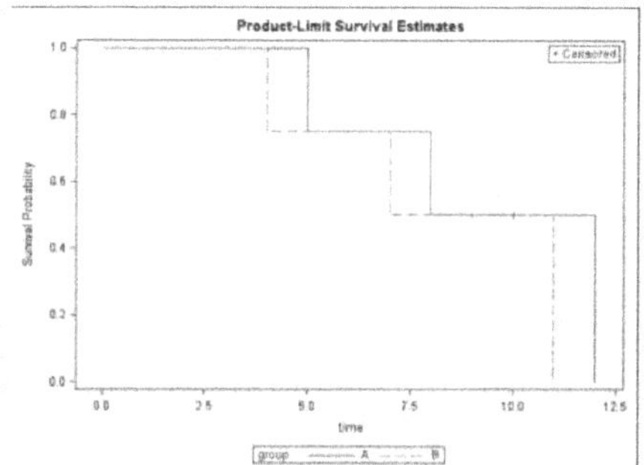

Interpretation:
SAS will generate Kaplan-Meier curves for each group (A and B),
which show the probability of survival over time.
Since KM is **non-parametric**, it doesn't make any assumptions
about the underlying distribution of survival times or
proportionality of hazards between groups.

2) The PROC PHREG procedure in SAS is used to perform **Cox proportional hazards regression,** a model designed for survival analysis.

Cox regression models the relationship between **the survival time and one or more predictor variables** (also called covariates) while assuming that the hazard ratios are constant over time (proportional hazards assumption).

time	censor	age	treatment
6	1	55	A
8	1	60	A
10	0	65	A
12	1	70	A
5	1	50	B
9	1	60	B
10	0	65	B
11	1	75	B

DATA Step: The dataset cox_data contains:

time: The time-to-event (survival time).
censor: The censoring variable where **1 indicates the event** (e.g., death), and 0 indicates censoring (no event).
age: A continuous variable representing the age of the subject.
treatment: A categorical variable indicating different treatment groups (A and B).

2) The PROC PHREG procedure in SAS is used to perform **Cox proportional hazards regression,** a model designed for survival analysis.

Cox regression models the relationship between **the survival time and one or more predictor variables** (also called covariates) while assuming that the hazard ratios are constant over time (proportional hazards assumption).

time	censor	age	treatment
6	1	55	A
8	1	60	A
10	0	65	A
12	1	70	A
5	1	50	B
9	1	60	B
10	0	65	B
11	1	75	B

DATA Step: The dataset cox_data contains:

time: The time-to-event (survival time).
censor: The censoring variable where **1 indicates the event** (e.g., death), and 0 indicates censoring (no event).
age: A continuous variable representing the age of the subject.
treatment: A categorical variable indicating different treatment groups (A and B).

time	censor	age	treatment
6	1	55	A
8	1	60	A
10	0	65	A
12	1	70	A
5	1	50	B
9	1	60	B
10	0	65	B
11	1	75	B

```
* Run PROC PHREG for Cox regression with CLASS statement for categorical
variable;
proc phreg data=cox_data;
    class treatment;                              /* Declare treatment as a
    categorical variable */
    model time*censor(0) = age treatment;    /* time is the survival time,
    censor is the censoring variable */
run;
```

model time*censor(0) = age treatment;: This defines the Cox model where time is the **survival time, and censor(0) indicates censored data. age and treatment are predictor variables (covariates).**

Parameter Estimates: These will include the regression coefficients for age and treatment.

Hazard Ratios: SAS will automatically provide hazard ratios (exponentiated coefficients) for each covariate in the model.

```
                   Analysis of Maximum Likelihood Estimates

                 Parameter    Standard                             Hazard
Parameter    DF    Estimate      Error    Chi-Square   Pr > ChiSq   Ratio   Label

age           1    -0.40676    0.21220     3.6743        0.0553     0.666
treatment A   1    -0.77331    1.26447     0.3740        0.5408     0.461   treatment A
```

- **Parameter Estimates**: Coefficients showing the effect of each variable on survival.

- **Hazard Ratios**: The risk of the event happening, with values >1 indicating higher risk and <1 indicating lower risk.

3) The PROC LIFEREG procedure in SAS is used for **parametric survival analysis**. Unlike PROC PHREG or PROC LIFETEST (which are non-parametric or semi-parametric),
PROC LIFEREG makes specific assumptions about the distribution of time-to-event data.
 This procedure allows you to model survival times using distributions such as **Weibull, Exponential, Lognormal,** etc.

Key Points:
Parametric Regression: This method assumes the survival times follow a specific distribution (e.g., Weibull, Exponential, or Lognormal).
Modeling Hazard/Survival Function: You can explicitly model the underlying survival function or hazard rate based on the assumed distribution.

time	censor	age	treatment
6	1	55	A
8	1	60	A
10	0	65	A
12	1	70	A
5	1	50	B
9	1	60	B
10	0	65	B
11	1	75	B

DATA Step:

time: The time-to-event (survival time).

censor: The censoring indicator (1 for event, 0 for censored).

age and treatment: Covariates where age is continuous, and treatment is categorical.

```
* Run PROC LIFEREG with Weibull distribution;
proc lifereg data=lifereg_data;
   class treatment;                             /* Declare
   treatment as categorical */
   model time*censor(0) = age treatment / dist=weibull;   /* Use
   Weibull distribution */
run;
```

PROC LIFEREG:

class treatment;: Declares the treatment variable as categorical.

model time*censor(0) = age treatment / dist=weibull;: This fits a parametric model to the data assuming a Weibull distribution for survival times.

You can replace weibull with other distributions like exponential, lognormal, etc.

Output:
- Parameter estimates for covariates (age, treatment) similar to those in linear regression.
- Estimates of the scale and shape parameters for the Weibull distribution (or whichever distribution you use).
- Hazard ratios are not directly provided, but you can calculate them based on the output.

```
                     Analysis of Maximum Likelihood Parameter Estimates

                                 Standard    95% Confidence     Chi-
         Parameter       DF Estimate   Error        Limits      Square  Pr > ChiSq

         Intercept        1  -0.4289  0.4856  -1.3806   0.5229    0.78    0.3771
         age              1   0.0427  0.0081   0.0269   0.0585   28.05    <.0001
         treatment    A   1  -0.0447  0.0798  -0.2012   0.1118    0.31    0.5756
         treatment    B   0   0.0000    .        .        .        .        .
         Scale            1   0.0892  0.0318   0.0444   0.1794
```

Hazard Ratio (95% CI): A measure of the risk of an event occurring in the treatment group compared to the control group, with a 95% confidence interval.

Hazard Ratio (95% CI): Suppose Drug A has a hazard ratio of 0.75 (0.60, 0.90).

This means that patients on Drug A have a 25% lower risk of the event (like disease progression) compared to the control group, with a 95% confidence interval ranging from 0.60 to 0.90.

If this interval doesn't include 1.0, the result is often considered statistically significant

P-value: The probability that the observed results are due to chance; values below 0.05 typically indicate statistical significance.

P-value: If the p-value is 0.03, there's a 3% probability that the observed difference between treatment and control groups happened by chance.

Because it's below 0.05, this result would be statistically significant, suggesting the treatment had a real effect.Median (95% CI): The middle value of survival time with a 95% confidence interval, indicating the range where the true median is likely to lie.**Median (95% CI)**: If the median survival time for Drug A is 15 months (12, 18), this means the typical survival time is 15 months, with a 95% confidence interval of 12 to 18 months, indicating the likely range of the true median.

Time to Event: The duration from a starting point (e.g., treatment start) to a specific event (e.g., death, relapse).

Time to Event: If a study starts on January 1 and the "time to event" for a patient is 10 months, that means the specific event (e.g., relapse or death) occurred around October 1.

```
libname adam "G:\My Journey Drive\YT ONCOLOGY DEPTH\Day-9-07sep2024";
/*N/BIGN counts from ADSL*/
proc sql noprint;
create table trt as
select trt01pn,trt01p,count (distinct usubjid) as denom
from adam.adsl
group by trt01pn,trt01p
order by trt01pn,trt01p;
select denom into: N1 - :N2 from trt;
quit;
run;
%put &N1 &N2;
/*Best Overall Response*/
data adrs;
merge adam.adrs (in=a drop=trt01p) adam.adsl;
by usubjid;
if a;
run;
proc sort;by trt01pn trt01p;
where aval ne .;run;
proc freq data=adrs;
by trt01pn trt01p;
tables aval*avalc/out=rs_aval (drop=percent);
run;
/*to get pct*/
proc sort data=rs_aval;by trt01pn trt01p;run;
proc sort data=trt;by trt01pn trt01p;run;
data pct;
length avalcc $200.;
merge rs_aval (in=a) trt (in=b);
by trt01pn trt01p;
pct=count/denom*100;
grp= put (count,4.)||" ("||put (pct,5.1)||")";
if avalc='CR' then avalcc=' Complete Response (CR)';
if avalc='PR' then avalcc=' Partial Response (PR)';
if avalc='PD' then avalcc=' Progressive Disease (PD)';
if avalc='SD' then avalcc=' Stable Disease (SD)';
run;
```

```
    data lbl;
length avalcc $200.;
avalcc='Best Overall Response';
aval=0;
run;
    data pct;
set lbl pct;
run;
proc sort;
by aval avalcc;
run;
proc transpose data=pct out=pct1;
var grp;
id trt01pn;
by aval avalcc;
run;

data sec1;
set pct1;
if aval gt 0 then do;
if _1='' then _1=' 0';
if _2='' then _2=' 0';end;
sec=1;
run;
    /*Best Objective Response (CR or PR)*/
    data adrs;
set adrs;
if aval in ( 1 2) then objrespfl=1;
else objrespfl=2;
run;
proc freq data=adrs;
by trt01pn trt01p;
tables objrespfl/out=rs0;
run;
    /*to get pct*/
proc sort data=rs0;by trt01pn trt01p;run;
proc sort data=trt;by trt01pn trt01p;run;
    data pct2;
length avalcc $200.;
merge rs0 (in=a) trt (in=b);
by trt01pn trt01p;
pct=count/denom*100;
grp= put (count,4.)||" ("||put (pct,5.1)||")";
if objrespfl=1 then avalcc='Best Objective Response (CR or PR)';
if objrespfl=1;
aval=1;
sec=2;
run;
```

```sas
proc sort;
by aval avalcc;
run;
proc transpose data=pct2 out=pct3;
var grp;
id trt01pn;
by aval avalcc sec;
run;
    data sec2;
set pct3;
run;
/*95% CI for Objective Response Rate*/
ods trace on;
ods output BinomialCLs=rs1;
proc freq data=adrs;
by trt01pn trt01p;
tables objrespfl/binomial (exact);
run;
    ods trace off;
    data rs11;
set rs1;
ci= put (LowerCL,6.4)||"-"||put (UpperCL,6.4);
avalcc=' 95% CI for Objective Response Rate';
aval=2;
sec=2;
run;
    proc sort;
by aval avalcc;
run;
proc transpose data=rs11 out=sec3;
var ci;
id trt01pn;
by aval avalcc sec;
run;
    /*Difference in Objective Response Rate*/
ods trace on;
ods output RiskDiffCol1=rs2;
ods output RiskDiffCol1=rs3;
proc freq data=adrs;
tables trt01pn*objrespfl/riskdiff;
run;
ods trace off;
    data sec4;
set rs2;
if row='Difference';
rr= put (Risk,6.4);
avalcc=' Difference in Objective Response Rate';
sec=2;
```

```sas
aval=3;
_3=rr;
run;
    data sec5;
set rs2;
if row='Difference';
_3=put (LowerCL,6.4)||"-"||put (UpperCL,6.4);
sec=2;
aval=4;
avalcc=' 95% CI for Objective Response Rate';
run;
    /* P-value*/
proc freq data=adrs;
tables trt01pn*objrespfl/cmh;
ods output cmh=cmh (where=( AltHypothesis="Row Mean Scores Differ"));
run;
    data sec6;
set cmh;
sec=2;
aval=5;
avalcc=' P-value';
_3= put (prob,6.4);
run;

data final;
set sec:;
keep sec aval avalcc _1 _2 _3;
run;
    %INCLUDE "G:\ONCO08_160820240600\Macro\RTF.SAS";
TITLE1 J=L "Genesis, Inc.";
TITLE2 J=L "Protocol#: MMSC 2023-01";
TITLE3 J=C "Summarize objective response rates";
    FOOTNOTE1 J=L "G:\PROJECT_2014\Project_2014\Pgm\T_14_1_111.SAS";
FOOTNOTE2 J=L "Complete Response (CR) Partial Response (PR) Stable Disease (SD) Progressive Disease (PD)
Not Applicable (NA)";
    OPTIONS ORIENTATION =LANDSCAPE;
ODS ESCAPECHAR='^';
ODS RTF FILE='G:\T_14_1_111.RTF' STYLE=Styles.Test;
PROC REPORT DATA=FINAL NOWD SPLIT='|' STYLE={OUTPUTWIDTH=100%};
COLUMN SEC AVAL AVALCC _1 _2 _3 ;
DEFINE SEC /ORDER NOPRINT;
DEFINE AVAL/ORDER NOPRINT;
DEFINE AVALCC / " "
STYLE (COLUMN)={JUST=L CELLWIDTH=35% ASIS=ON}
STYLE (HEADER)={JUST=L CELLWIDTH=35% ASIS=ON};

DEFINE _1 / "DRUG A|(N=&N1)"
STYLE (COLUMN)={JUST=L CELLWIDTH=20% ASIS=ON}
```

```
STYLE (HEADER)={JUST=L CELLWIDTH=20% ASIS=ON};

DEFINE _2 / "DRUG B|(N=&N2)"
STYLE (COLUMN)={JUST=L CELLWIDTH=20% ASIS=ON}
STYLE (HEADER)={JUST=L CELLWIDTH=20% ASIS=ON};
    DEFINE _3 / "Treatment Comparison"
STYLE (COLUMN)={JUST=L CELLWIDTH=24% ASIS=ON}
STYLE (HEADER)={JUST=L CELLWIDTH=24% ASIS=ON};

COMPUTE BEFORE _PAGE_;
LINE@1 "^{STYLE [OUTPUTWIDTH=100% BORDERTOPWIDTH=0.5PT]}";
ENDCOMP;
    COMPUTE AFTER _PAGE_;
LINE@1 "^{STYLE [OUTPUTWIDTH=100% BORDERTOPWIDTH=0.5PT]}";
ENDCOMP;
COMPUTE BEFORE SEC;
LINE ";
ENDCOMP;
RUN;
ODS _ALL_ CLOSE;
```

```
                                                            00:00 Wednesday, September 3, 2014  1

PHARMA Private Limited.
Protocol: 043-1-2025
                              Table 14.1.7 Summarize objective response rates
```

	DRUG A (N=4)	DRUG B (N=3)	Treatment Comparison
Best Overall Response			
Complete Response (CR)	1 (25.0)	0	
Partial Response (PR)	2 (50.0)	0	
Stable Disease (SD)	0	1 (33.3)	
Progressive Disease (PD)	1 (25.0)	0	
Best Objective Response (CR or PR)	3 (75.0)		
95% CI for Objective Response Rate	0.1941-0.993	0.0250-1.000	
Difference in Objective Response Rate			0.7500
95% CI for Objective Response Rate			0.3257-1.0000
P-value			0.2207

Time-to-Event (TTE) Analyses in Clinical Trials

Time-to-event analyses, also known as survival analyses, are commonly used in clinical trials to evaluate how long it takes for a particular event (such as disease progression or death) to occur after a patient begins treatment.

Common Examples of Time-to-Event Endpoints:

Overall Survival (OS): Time from randomization until death from any cause.

Progression-Free Survival (PFS): Time from randomization until either disease progression or death.

Time to Progression (TTP): Time from randomization until disease progression, ignoring death.

Kaplan-Meier Estimation:

The Kaplan-Meier (KM) method is used to estimate the probability of surviving beyond certain time points. For example, suppose we are evaluating PFS:

If the median PFS in the placebo group is 6 months and in the treatment group it is 9 months, this means 50% of patients in the treatment group are progression-free at 9 months, compared to only 6 months in the placebo group.

Confidence intervals (usually 95%) are calculated for these medians to show the precision of the estimate.

Comparing Treatment Arms: Log-Rank Test

To statistically compare the treatment and placebo arms, a log-rank test is used:

If p-value < 0.05, the difference in survival curves is considered statistically significant.

For example, if the p-value for comparing PFS is 0.03, we conclude that the treatment significantly prolongs progression-free survival compared to placebo.

Hazard Ratio (HR): Cox Proportional Hazards Model

The hazard ratio (HR), estimated using a Cox regression model, quantifies the risk of the event in the treatment group relative to the placebo:

An HR of 0.70 implies a 30% reduction in the risk of event (e.g., death or progression) in the treatment group.

An HR < 1 favors the treatment, while > 1 favors the placebo.

Example:

Let's say:

trt01pn = 1 represents Treatment

trt01pn = 2 represents Placebo

Using these values in the Cox model:

proc phreg data=adam.adtte; class stratvar; model aval*cnsr(1) = trt01pn / ties=efron; strata stratvar; run;

The hazard ratio is interpreted relative to the reference group. If placebo (2) is the reference, and HR = 0.70, the treatment reduces the risk by 30%.

If treatment (1) is set as the reference by mistake, the HR might come out as 1.43, suggesting a misleading result unless correctly interpreted.

Importance of Correct Reference Group:

Always verify how the treatment groups are coded and review footnotes in the mock shells or TFLs, which clarify:

What is considered the reference group?

How is HR calculated?

Any misinterpretation here could lead to incorrect conclusions about the efficacy of the treatment.

Mock Table Overview

This is a typical summary table used in efficacy analysis for survival endpoints like:

Overall Survival (OS)

Progression-Free Survival (PFS)

Time to Progression (TTP)

Table Columns:

Metric	Drug A	Placebo	Treatment Comparison
Median (95% CI)	XX (XX,XX)	XX (XX,XX)	
P-value			XXX
Hazard Ratio (95%CI)			XX (XX,XX)

? Explanation of SAS Code

The code is divided into two parts:

KM Estimates and Log-Rank Test (Median & P-value)

Cox Regression for Hazard Ratio

? 1. KM Estimates and Log-Rank Test

** Median survival time and p-value **; ods listing close; ods output Quartiles=quart (keep=trt01pn estimate lowerlimit upperlimit percent) HomTests=pval (keep=pTest probchisq where=(test="Log-Rank")); proc lifetest data=adtte; time aval*cnsr(1); strata trt01pn; run; ods output close; ods listing;

? Explanation:

proc lifetest: Performs Kaplan-Meier survival analysis.

time aval*cnsr(1): aval is the time variable; cnsr=1 indicates censored observations.

strata trt01pn: Compares KM curves across treatment groups.

ods output:

Quartiles dataset captures median survival time and its CI (for Percent=50).

HomTests dataset captures log-rank test p-value to compare survival curves.

Example Interpretation:

Median PFS: Drug A = 9.2 months (CI: 8.3–10.1), Placebo = 6.1 months (CI: 5.3–7.2)

Log-rank p-value = 0.004 (statistically significant)

? 2. Cox Proportional Hazards Model for Hazard Ratio

** Hazard ratio **; ods listing close; ods output parameterestimates=hrdata (keep=hazardratio hrlowercl hruppercl); proc phreg data=adtte; class trt01pn; model aval*cnsr(1)=trt01pn / ties=discrete risklimits; hazardratio trt01pn; run; ods output close; ods listing;

? Explanation:

proc phreg: Fits the Cox proportional hazards model.

model aval*cnsr(1)=trt01pn: Computes the hazard ratio between treatment arms.

hazardratio trt01pn: Displays HR with 95% CI.

ties=discrete: Method to handle tied event times.

Example Interpretation:

Hazard Ratio (Drug A vs Placebo) = 0.65 (95% CI: 0.52–0.81)

Interpreted as 35% risk reduction for progression/death in Drug A vs Placebo.

?? Important Note on trt01pn:

Ensure:

Drug A = 1, Placebo = 2 (or vice versa) is used consistently.

Changing the coding flips the interpretation of hazard ratio (e.g., HR = 0.65 vs 1.54).

Time to Disease Progression Using NADIR (Example: PSA)

In oncology trials, time to disease progression can be defined using a Nadir-based rule, especially for biomarkers like Prostate-Specific Antigen (PSA) in prostate cancer.

? What is NADIR?

Nadir is the lowest observed value of a lab test (e.g., PSA) after baseline.

It's recalculated at each time point, using only the past values, to evaluate changes relative to the best previous response.

? How is PSA Progression Defined?

A typical definition could be:

PSA progression occurs when a patient's PSA increases ≥30% above the Nadir, and

This increase is confirmed at the next visit with another value also ≥30% above the Nadir.

? Event Date (ADT):

Defined as the date of first confirmed PSA progression, based on the above condition.

? Annotated SAS Code Walkthrough

1. Create Raw PSA Dataset

data psa; format RANDDT mmddyy10.; input USUBJID $ 1-3 AVISIT $ 5-12 AVISITN LBDTC $ 17-26 PSA; retain BASE; RANDDT='15SEP2018'd; /* Randomization Date */ if avisitn=0 then base=psa; /* Store baseline */ if avisitn > 0 then postbfl=1; else postbfl=0; datalines; 101 BASELINE 0 2018-09-21 23.31 101 WEEK 1 1 2018-09-27 44.65 101 WEEK 4 2 2018-10-09 21.78 101 WEEK 9 3 2018-11-13 13.96 101 WEEK 15 4 2018-12-27 31.34 101 WEEK 19 5

2019-01-23 26.51 ; run; proc sort data=psa; by usubjid postbfl; run;

2. Derive Nadir (Lowest PSA up to Current Point)

data psa; set psa; by usubjid postbfl; retain NADIR; if first.usubjid then nadir=.; lagpsa = lag(psa); if postbfl then do; if first.postbfl then nadir = base; else nadir = min(nadir, lagpsa); end; if postbfl and psa ne . then do; chg_nadir = psa - nadir; if nadir ne 0 then pchg_nadir = chg_nadir / nadir * 100; end; run;

This calculates:

NADIR: Minimum prior PSA

pchg_nadir: Percent change from NADIR

3. Flag Potential and Confirmed Progression

data psa; set psa; retain nextge30pct_nadir; by usubjid avisitn; ge30pct_nadir = (pchg_nadir >= 30); nextge30pct_nadir = lag(ge30pct_nadir); run;

ge30pct_nadir: Indicates current visit has PSA increase ≥30% over Nadir

nextge30pct_nadir: Indicates previous visit also had ≥30% increase (confirmation)

4. Create ADaM-style Time-to-Event Dataset

data adpsa; format adt date9.; set psa; if ge30pct_nadir and nextge30pct_nadir; /* Confirmed progression */ ADT = input(lbdtc, yymmdd10.); AVAL = (ADT - RANDDT + 1) / 30.4375; /* Time in months */ EVNTDESC = 'PSA Progression'; CNSR = 0; keep usubjid lbdtc adt randdt aval evntdesc cnsr; run;

ADT: Date of confirmed PSA progression

AVAL: Time to event (in months)

CNSR: Censor flag (0 = event occurred)

? Example Interpretation

For Subject 101:

Baseline PSA = 23.31

Nadir = 13.96 (at WEEK 9)

WEEK 15 PSA = 31.34 → 124% ↑ from Nadir

WEEK 19 PSA = 26.51 → 89.9% ↑ from Nadir

→ Both increases are ≥30% → Confirmed progression → ADT = 2019-01-23

Obs	USUBJID	RANDDT	AVISIT	AVISITN	LBDTC	PSA	BASE	postbfl	NADIR	lagpsa	chg_nadir	pchg_nadir	ge30pct_nadir	nextge30pct_nadir
1	101	09/15/2018	BASELINE	0	2018-09-21	23.31	23.31	0	.	.	.	.	0	.
2	101	09/15/2018	WEEK 1	1	018-09-27	44.65	23.31	1	23.31	23.31	21.34	91.540	1	0
3	101	09/15/2018	WEEK 4	2	018-10-09	21.78	23.31	1	23.31	44.65	-1.53	-6.564	0	1
4	101	09/15/2018	WEEK 9	3	018-11-13	13.96	23.31	1	21.78	21.78	-7.82	-35.904	0	0
5	101	09/15/2018	WEEK 15	4	018-12-27	31.34	23.31	1	13.96	13.96	17.38	124.499	1	0
6	101	09/15/2018	WEEK 19	5	019-01-23	26.51	23.31	1	13.96	31.34	12.55	89.900	1	1

Figure 6 is a time-to-event analysis dataset based on the example dataset in Figure 5

Obs	USUBJID	LBDTC	ADT	RANDDT	AVAL	EVNTDESC	CNSR
1	101	2019-01-23	23JAN2019	09/15/2018	4.30390	PSA Progression	0

Figure 6 Analysis Dataset for Time to PSA Progression

ANALYSES ON FOLLOW-UP TIME

To estimate the follow-up time between two treatment arms, the median follow-up time can be estimated by Reverse Kaplan-Meier as mentioned above. An example summary table to present summary statistics is shown below:

Figure 7 is a sample mock-up for follow-up time.

	Drug A	Placebo
Follow-up Time Based on Reverse Kaplan-Meier Estimates		
n	XXX	XXX
25th Percentile	XXX	XXX
Median	XXX	XXX
75th Percentile	XXX	XXX

Figure 7 Mock-up Table for Follow-up Time

```
    /* Step 1: Get total number of subjects per treatment arm */
proc means data=adeff nway noprint;
var aval;
class trt01pn;
output out=tot n=n;
run;
    proc sort data=tot;
by trt01pn;
run;
    proc transpose data=tot out=tran_tot (drop=_label_
rename=(_name_=name _1=drug_A _2=placebo));
id trt01pn;
var n;
run;
    /* Step 2: Macro to get the reverse KM percentiles (i.e., median follow-up time) */
%macro reverse_km(num=, dsout=);
ods listing close;
    ods output Lifetest.Stratum&num..TimeSummary.Quartiles = &dsout.;
    proc lifetest data=adeff;
time aval*cnsr(0); /* Reverse KM: treat censored = 1 as events */
strata trt01pn;
run;
    ods output close;
ods listing;
    proc sort data=&dsout.;
by percent;
```

```
run;
%mend;
    /* Step 3: Call macro for each group */
%reverse_km(num=1, dsout=trt1);
%reverse_km(num=2, dsout=trt2);
```

data percent; merge trt1(keep=percent estimate rename=(estimate = drug_A)) trt2(keep=percent estimate rename=(estimate = placebo)); by percent; rename percent=col1; run;

Explanation:

cnsr(0): Reverses censoring—so the originally censored subjects are now treated as if they had an "event" (e.g., dropped from follow-up).

This allows estimation of median follow-up time instead of event time (i.e., how long patients were observed before censoring).

This method is referenced in oncology studies to describe adequacy of follow-up using reverse Kaplan-Meier.

CHAPTER THREE

GRAPHICAL ANALYSIS

Common Graphical Analysis Techniques in SAS

1. Kaplan-Meier (KM) Curve

KM curves are commonly used to compare the survival experience between two treatment arms.

They provide a visual representation of the proportion of patients who remain event-free over time.

A summary table of patients at risk is usually displayed alongside the KM curve.

"At risk" refers to patients who have not experienced the event of interest (e.g., disease progression) or have not been censored.

The SAS option ATRISK is used to display the number of patients still at risk at different time points.

Figure 8 illustrates an example of a Kaplan-Meier curve.

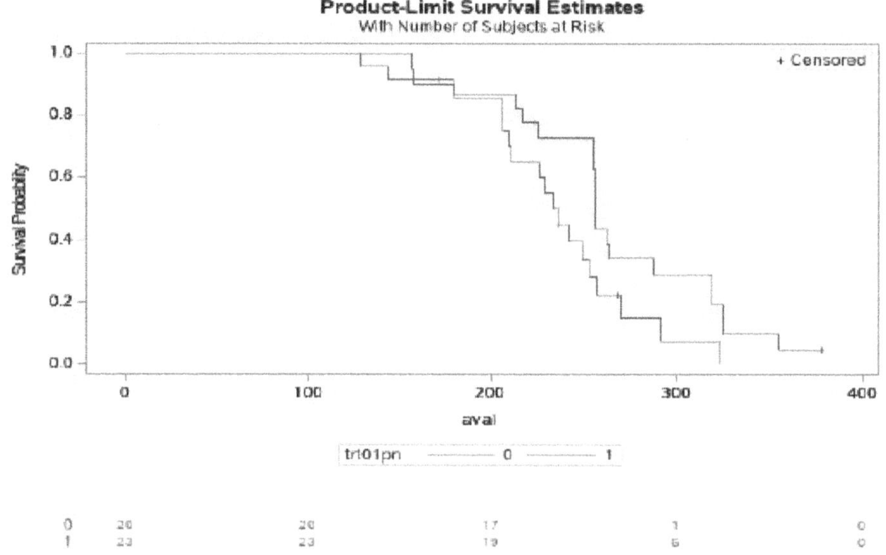

Figure 8 Example of KM Curve

ods graphics on;
ods output ProductlimitEstimates = _ple
Quartiles = _quart
CensoredSummary = _cs
Survivalplot = _splot
homtests = pval;
***_ple: Event/Cum. Event*
_quart: estimate of the median survival time

_cs: censored summary
_splot: info about patient at risk
pval: p-value based on log rank test;
proc lifetest data=adttee method=km plots=(survival(atrisk (outside(0.15))) LS);
11
*time aval*cnsr(1);*
strata trt01pn;
run;
ods output close;
ods graphics off;

ODS Output Datasets:
_ple: Contains event and cumulative event counts.
_quart: Provides the estimated median survival time.
_cs: Includes summary details about censored patients.
_splot: Holds data used to generate the survival plot (e.g., number at risk).
pval: Contains p-values from the log-rank test.
LIFETEST Procedure Breakdown:
data=adttee: Specifies the input ADaM dataset.
method=km: Uses the Kaplan-Meier estimation method.
plots=survival(...): Requests a survival curve with:
atrisk(outside(0.15)): Displays the number at risk below the plot, offset by 15%.
LS: Produces line and step plot for survival.
time aval*cnsr(1):
aval: Time to event variable.
cnsr(1): Censoring indicator, where 1 = censored.
strata trt01pn: Compares survival curves by treatment group (trt01pn).
Important Notes for Validating Kaplan-Meier (KM) Curves
Carefully review the shape of KM curves during validation.
Ensure the legend labels correctly correspond to the plotted treatment groups.
When the hazard ratio (HR) relative to placebo is less than 1:
This indicates lower risk in the treatment arm compared to placebo.
Therefore, the KM curve for the treatment arm is expected to lie above the placebo curve (indicating better survival or delayed event occurrence).
This visual alignment between hazard ratio interpretation and KM curves is a critical validation checkpoint.
? What is the Assumption of Proportional Hazards?
In Cox regression, we assume that:
The risk (hazard) of an event is always proportional between groups over time.
In other words:
If Treatment A has twice the risk of Treatment B at the beginning,
It should still be twice the risk later on — the ratio (hazard ratio) stays constant over time.
? How to Check This Assumption?
We use graphs to visually inspect this assumption. Two common plots are:
$-\log(S(t))$ vs time (t)
$\log(-\log(S(t)))$ vs $\log(t)$
If the lines are roughly parallel, the assumption holds.
If the lines cross or curve differently, the assumption may not hold.

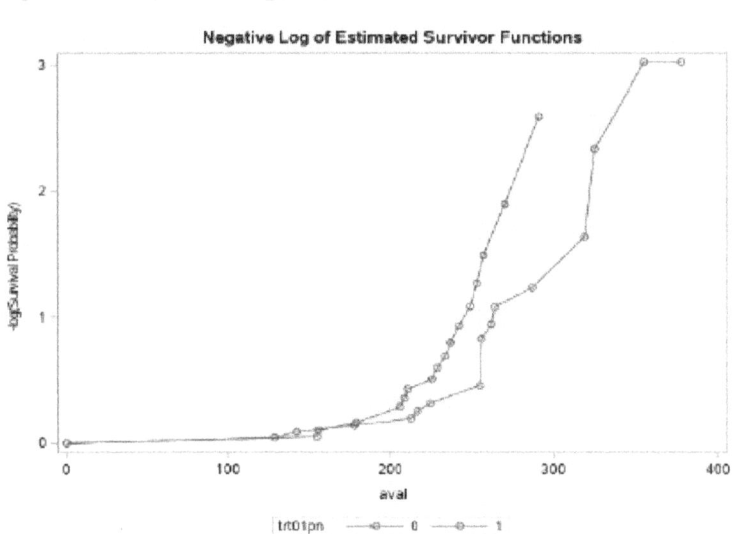

The image shows:

➤ Plot of -log(S(t)) vs time

Blue line: One treatment group

Red line: Another treatment group

? Observation:

The lines are not straight and not parallel.

? Interpretation:

This suggests that the hazards are not proportional. The treatment effect may change over time, violating the assumption.

? Real-life Example:

Imagine we're testing two drugs for heart disease:

Drug A and Placebo

If the hazard of death for Drug A is always 50% of Placebo from start to end, the assumption holds.

But if Drug A starts strong but later becomes less effective, the assumption is violated.

Let me generate a custom visual that clearly shows this idea with two examples — one where the assumption holds and one where it doesn't.

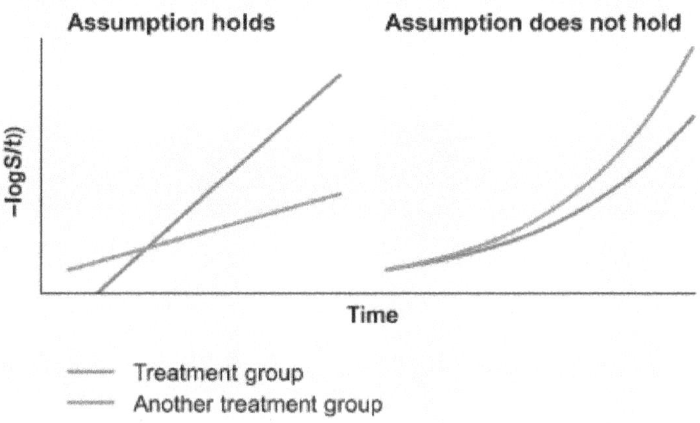

? What is a Waterfall Plot?

A waterfall plot is used in oncology to show how much tumor size (or any marker like PSA) increased or decreased for each patient.

Each vertical bar = one subject

X-axis = subjects sorted by response (worst to best)

Y-axis = % change from baseline (e.g. PSA)

If a bar goes down (negative), it means the subject responded well (e.g., PSA dropped).

If a bar goes up, it means no improvement or worsening.

? Example Dataset (adpsa)

This dataset has:

SUBJID – Subject ID

PCHG – % change from baseline in PSA

TRT01PN – Treatment arm (1 or 2)

SUBJID PCHG TRT01PN

1001 -86.56 1

1002 -95.23 1

1004 -93.31 2

...

Subjects may have multiple PSA values — we need the best (lowest) per subject.

? Data Preparation Summary

/* Step 1: Sort by subject and PCHG */ proc sort data = adpsa; by subjid pchg; where PCHG ne . ; run; /* Step 2: Keep only the best PSA change (first.pchg per subject) */ data adpsa; set adpsa; by subjid pchg; if first.subjid; run; /* Step 3: Sort to order subjects by PCHG */ proc sort; by trt01pn descending pchg; run; /* Step 4: Assign subject order */ data bestpsa_; set adpsa; n = _n_; run;

? Plot Creation

proc sgplot data = bestpsa_; vbar n / response=pchg group=trt01pn;

vbar creates vertical bars

n is the x-axis subject order

pchg is the bar height (% change)

group=trt01pn shows color by treatment

? Final Output

The plot shows:

Subjects on the x-axis

Best % PSA change on the y-axis

Bars grouped (colored) by treatment arm

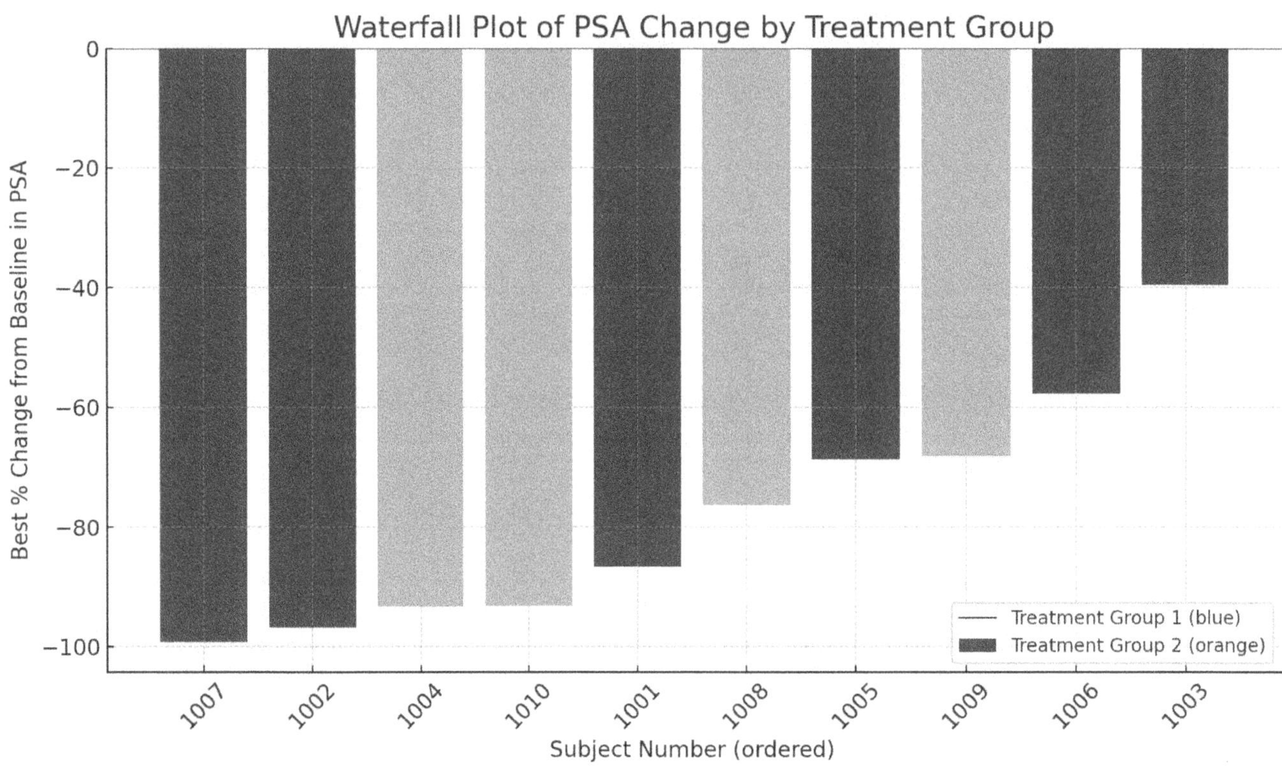

Here is the Waterfall Plot generated based on your dataset. Each bar represents the best PSA change from baseline for one subject:

Blue bars = Treatment Group 1

Orange bars = Treatment Group 2

Lower bars (more negative) indicate better tumor/PSA reduction

This graph helps you:

Spot how each treatment performs

See how many subjects had tumor shrinkage (bars below 0)

Visualize best responses across treatment groups

Bar Chart

Bar charts are a great way to display categorical data and summarize the frequency and percentage for each category. For example, we can summarize the best overall response in a bar chart (shown below) and add a summary table in the legend to display the statistics of the objective response rate.

Figure 11 is a bar chart summarizing the best overall response for Drug vs. Placebo

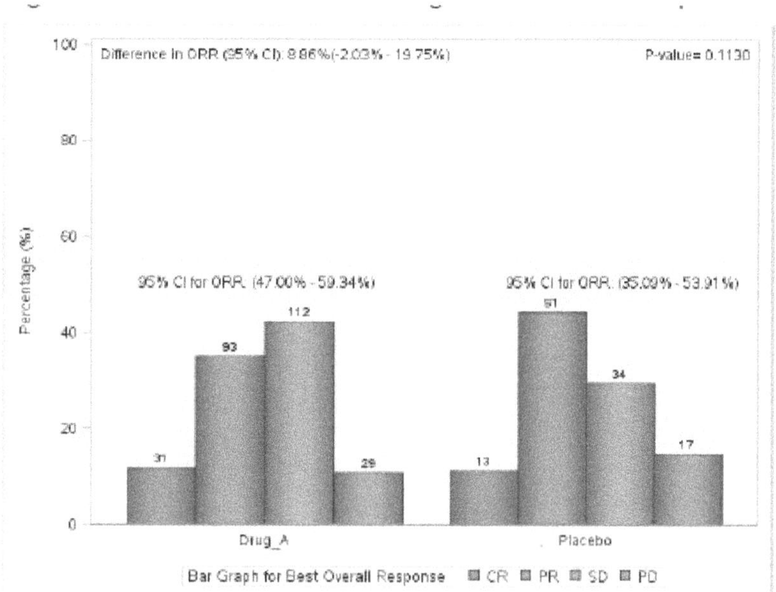

Figure 11 Bar Chart for Drug vs. Placebo

```
    data adpsa;
input trt01p $10. aval $ count;
datalines;
Drug_A CR 31
Drug_A PR 93
Drug_A SD 112
Drug_A PD 29
Placebo CR 13
Placebo PR 51
Placebo SD 34
Placebo PD 17
;
run;
proc sql noprint;
select sum(count) into: trt1 from adpsa where trt01p='Drug_A';
select sum(count) into: trt2 from adpsa where trt01p='Placebo';
quit;
%let trt1=&trt1; %let trt2=&trt2;
%put trt1=&trt1, trt2=&trt2;
data cat;
set adpsa;
if trt01p='Drug_A' then percent = round(count/&trt1*100, .1);
if trt01p='Placebo' then percent = round(count/&trt2*100, .1);
run;
proc sgplot data=cat;
vbar trt01p/group=aval response=percent groupdisplay=cluster grouporder=data
dataskin=pressed attrid=aval datalabel=count;
```

```
xaxis display=(nolabel noticks);
yaxis values=(0 to 100 by 20) label='Percentage (%)';
keylegend/title='Best Overall Response'
title = 'Bar Graph for Best Overall Response'; inset "P-value= &pval"/position=topright; inset "Difference in ORR
(95% CI): &df" /position=topleft; inset " 95% CI for ORR: &ORR1 " /position=left; inset "95% CI for ORR: &ORR2 "
/position=right; *&df, &pval, &ORR1, &ORR2 correspond to the statistics in Figure 3*;
run;
```

Mean Standard Error Plot

The plot of mean change over time is commonly used in conjunction with standard error bars. In a mean standard error plot, the X-axis represents time and the Y-axis represents the overall mean. Each point on the graph represents the overall mean value of the data at a specific time point and is associated with an error bar. The bar above the point is computed by adding one standard error while the bar below the point is computed by subtracting one standard error. The mean plots visualize the shift in mean over time and the error bars display the overall distribution of the data.

Figure 12 is an example of Mean Standard Error plot

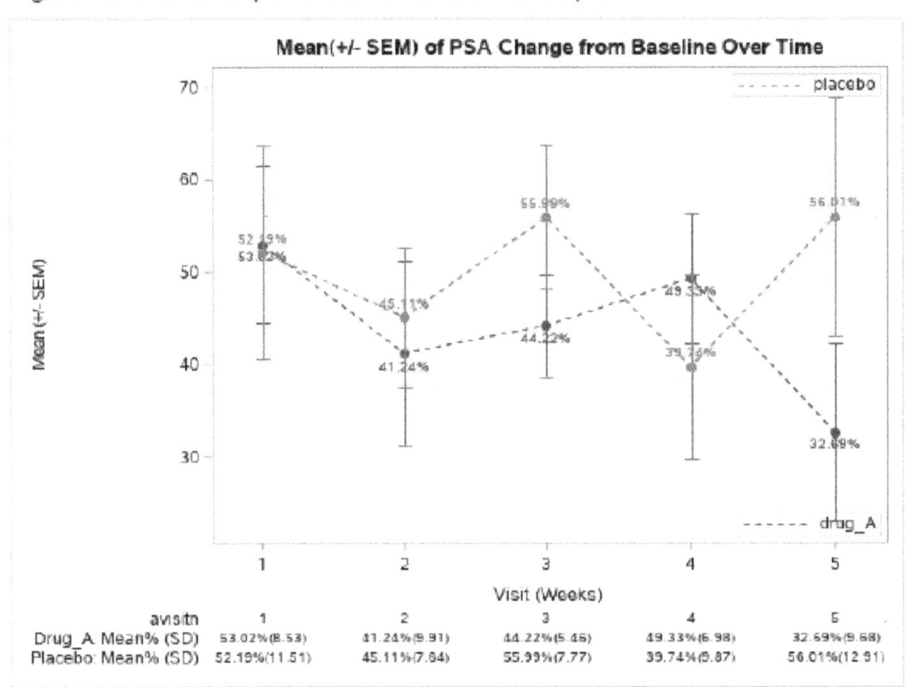

Figure 12 Mean Standard Error Plot of Drug vs. Placebo

```
/* Create sample data */
data adpsa(drop=i);
length trt01p $100;
do trt01p = 'drug_A', 'placebo';
do i = 1 to 10;
do avisitn = 1 to 5;
psapchg = ranuni(0) * 100;
output;
end;
end;
```

```
end;
run;
    proc sort data=adpsa;
by trt01p avisitn;
run;
    /* Macro to calculate mean and standard error */
%macro meanout(trt=, out=);
proc means data=adpsa noprint;
where trt01p = "&trt";
by trt01p avisitn;
var psapchg;
output out=meanout(drop=_type_ _freq_)
mean = &out._mean
stderr = &out._stderr;
run;
    data &out.;
set meanout;
&out._ll = &out._mean - &out._stderr;
&out._ul = &out._mean + &out._stderr;
run;
    proc sort data=&out.;
by avisitn;
run;
%mend;
    /* Generate mean and stderr for each treatment group */
%meanout(trt=drug_A, out=trt1);
%meanout(trt=placebo, out=trt2);
    /* Merge results and create display labels */
data master;
merge trt1(drop=trt01p) trt2(drop=trt01p);
by avisitn;
seq + 1;
    if trt1_mean ne . then
trt1_msd = strip(put(trt1_mean, 8.2)) || '%(' || strip(put(trt1_stderr, 8.2)) || ')';
    if trt2_mean ne . then
trt2_msd = strip(put(trt2_mean, 8.2)) || '%(' || strip(put(trt2_stderr, 8.2)) || ')';
    trt1_meanp = strip(put(trt1_mean, 8.2)) || '%';
trt2_meanp = strip(put(trt2_mean, 8.2)) || '%';
run;
    /* Plotting the graph */
proc sgplot data=master noautolegend;
series x=avisitn y=trt1_mean /
lineattrs=(color=blue pattern=2)
datalabel=trt1_meanp
datalabelpos=bottom
datalabelattrs=(color=blue)
name='drug_A'
legendlabel='drug_A';
```

```
    series x=avisitn y=trt2_mean /
lineattrs=(color=red pattern=2)
datalabel=trt2_meanp
datalabelpos=top
datalabelattrs=(color=red)
name='placebo'
legendlabel='placebo';
    scatter x=avisitn y=trt1_mean /
yerrorlower=trt1_ll
yerrorupper=trt1_ul
markerattrs=(color=blue symbol=CircleFilled)
errorbarattrs=(color=blue);
    scatter x=avisitn y=trt2_mean /
yerrorlower=trt2_ll
yerrorupper=trt2_ul
markerattrs=(color=red symbol=CircleFilled)
errorbarattrs=(color=red);
    xaxistable avisitn / x=seq location=outside;
xaxistable trt1_msd / x=seq location=outside label='Drug_A: Mean% (SD)';
xaxistable trt2_msd / x=seq location=outside label='Placebo: Mean% (SD)';
    yaxis label='Mean (+/- SEM)';
xaxis label='Visit (Weeks)';
title1 'Mean(+/- SEM) of PSA Change from Baseline Over Time';
    keylegend 'drug_A' / location=inside position=bottomright;
keylegend 'placebo' / location=inside position=topright;
run;
```

Spaghetti Plot

A spaghetti plot looks like a plate of spaghetti. It's a line plot displaying the trend for each individual subject. Each line in a spaghetti plot represents the change in value for one patient over multiple visits. The example code below shows how to generate a PSA spaghetti plot using the SGPLOT procedure with the dummy data.

Figure 13 is an example of spaghetti plot.

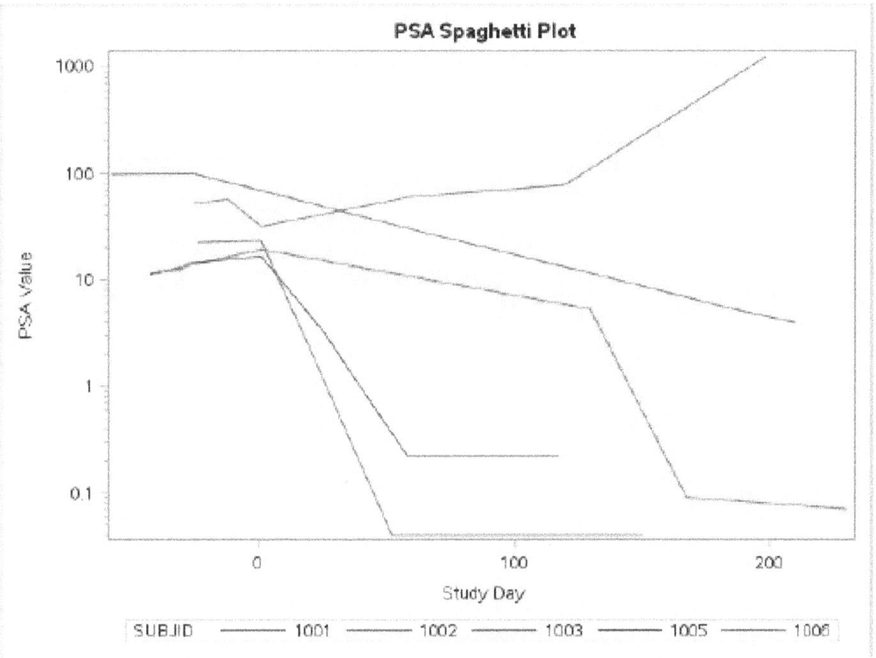

Figure 13 PSA Spaghetti Plot

```
    /* Input PSA data */
data adpsa;
format SUBJID z4.;
input SUBJID ADY AVAL TRT01PN;
PARAMCD = 'PSA';
datalines;
1001 -24 22.41 1
1001 1 23.22 1
1001 52 0.04 1
1001 150 0.04 1
1002 -25 52.01 1
1002 -12 56.78 1
1002 1 31.52 1
1002 58 59.21 1
1002 119 77.39 1
1002 198 1230.34 1
1003 -29 12.85 1
1003 -42 11.34 1
1003 1 19.21 1
1003 129 5.33 1
1003 167 0.09 1
1003 231 0.07 1
1005 -29 14.21 1
1005 1 16.54 1
```

```
1005 25 3.26 1
1005 58 0.22 1
1005 117 0.22 1
1006 -57 98.23 1
1006 -25 99.22 1
1006 54 32.11 1
1006 187 5.21 1
1006 210 3.94 1
;
run;
    /* Generate Spaghetti Plot */
proc sgplot data=adpsa(where=(trt01pn=1));
title 'PSA Spaghetti Plot';
series x=ady y=aval / group=subjid;
yaxis label='PSA Value'
type=log
logbase=10
logstyle=logexpand
minor;
xaxis label='Study Day';
run;
```

Forest Plot

Forest plots are commonly used to visualize statistical results for subgroup analysis in randomized controlled trials. The general structure of a forest plot consists of three parts: subgroup labels, plots of hazard ratios with associated confidence intervals, and relevant summary statistics.

The relevant statistics are summarized in the statistics panel in the plot. The statistics can be, for instance, number of patients and number of events for treatment versus placebo, hazard ratio with corresponding confidence interval, and p-value. It's important to note that in the plot panel of a forest plot the dots represent treatment effects, for instance, measured by hazard ratios in the Figure 14 below. Hazard ratios typically display as dots or diamond along with the corresponding confidence intervals: the amount of variation for the estimates of hazard ratio. The vertical line (x=1.0) in the middle indicates a hazard ratio of 0, which suggests no treatment effects. With placebo as reference group, a hazard ratio less than one indicates favoring treatment over placebo and the dot falls into the left-hand side of the plot panel. When validating forest plots, programmers need to cross-check with summary tables and assure that the statistics in the plot aligns with the statistics in the tables.

The example code below illustrates how to pre-summarize the statistics before creating a forest plot and how to create a plot with the SGPLOT procedure based on the pre-summarized data.

Figure 14 is an example of forest plot.

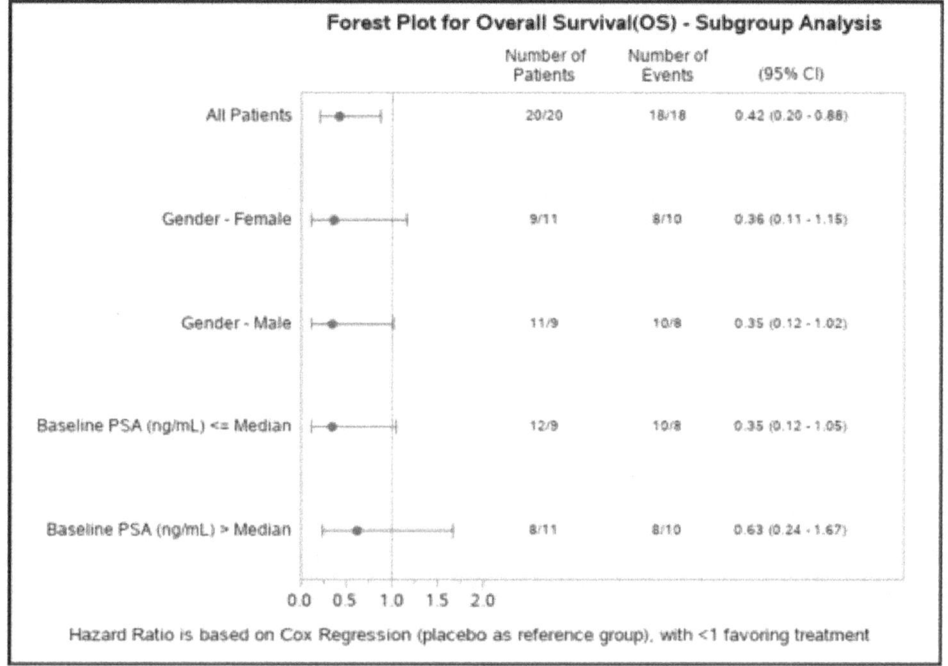

Figure 14 Forest Plot for Subgroup Analysis

Enter Caption

```
    /* Sample data */
data adeff;
input aval cnsr trtpn Sex $ tglscor psablmgr $ @@;
datalines;
179 0 1 F 6 Y 378 1 1 M 6 Y 256 0 1 F 9 Y 355 0 1 M 5 Y
262 0 1 M 7 N 319 0 1 M 8 N 256 0 1 F 7 Y 256 0 1 M 9 N
255 0 1 M 8 N 171 0 1 F 7 Y 224 1 1 F 9 Y 325 0 1 M 8 N
;
run;
    /* Forest plot macro */
%macro m_forestplot(indata=, llabel=, orderid=, var=);
    ods graphics on;
ods output Quartiles=_quart_&var CensoredSummary=_cs_&var;
    /* Kaplan-Meier estimates */
proc lifetest data=&indata plots=none;
time aval*cnsr(1);
strata trtpn;
run;
    ods output close;
ods graphics off;
    /* Get number of patients */
data cs_&var(keep=trtpn npatients);
```

```sas
set _cs_&var(where=(trtpn in (1,2)));
length npatients $25;
npatients = strip(put(total, best.));
run;
    proc transpose data=cs_&var out=_tcs_&var prefix=_;
var npatients;
id trtpn;
run;
    data tcs_&var(keep=orderid col0 col1);
set _tcs_&var;
length col0 col1 $200;
orderid = input(&orderid, best.);
col0 = &llabel.;
col1 = catx('/', _1, _2);
run;
    /* Get number of events */
data ecs_&var(keep=trtpn nevents);
set _cs_&var(where=(trtpn in (1,2)));
length nevents $25;
nevents = strip(put(failed, best.));
run;
    proc transpose data=ecs_&var out=_etcs_&var prefix=_;
var nevents;
id trtpn;
run;
    data etcs_&var(keep=orderid col0 col2);
set _etcs_&var;
length col0 col2 $200;
orderid = input(&orderid, best.);
col0 = &llabel.;
col2 = catx('/', _1, _2);
run;
    /* Cox model - Hazard Ratio */
ods output ParameterEstimates=_hzdata_&var;
proc phreg data=&indata;
class trtpn;
model aval*cnsr(1) = trtpn / ties=discrete risklimits;
run;
    data hzdata_&var(keep=orderid col0 or lcl ucl col3 HazardRatio HRLowerCL HRUpperCL);
set _hzdata_&var;
length col0 col3 $200;
orderid = input(&orderid, best.);
col0 = &llabel.;
or = HazardRatio;
lcl = HRLowerCL;
ucl = HRUpperCL;
col3 = strip(put(HazardRatio, 8.2)) || '(' || strip(put(HRLowerCL, 8.2)) || '-' || strip(put(HRUpperCL, 8.2)) || ')';
run;
```

```
    /* Combine all results */
data final_&var;
merge tcs_&var etcs_&var hzdata_&var;
by orderid;
run;
    %mend m_forestplot;
    /* Macro calls for subgroups */
%m_forestplot(indata=adeff, llabel='All Patients', orderid=1, var=allsubj);
%m_forestplot(indata=adeff(where=(sex='F')), llabel='Gender - Female', orderid=2, var=sexf);
%m_forestplot(indata=adeff(where=(sex='M')), llabel='Gender - Male', orderid=3, var=sexm);
%m_forestplot(indata=adeff(where=(psablmgr='Y')), llabel='Baseline PSA <= Median', orderid=4, var=psablmgry);
%m_forestplot(indata=adeff(where=(psablmgr='N')), llabel='Baseline PSA > Median', orderid=5, var=psablmgrn);
    /* Combine all results */
data master;
set final_allsubj final_sexf final_sexm final_psablmgry final_psablmgrn;
run;
    data master;
set master(keep=orderid col0 col1 col2 col3 HazardRatio HRLowerCL HRUpperCL);
length col11 col12 col13 $30;
col11 = 'Number of Patients';
col12 = 'Number of Events';
col13 = '(95% CI)';
run;
    proc sort data=master;
by descending orderid;
run;
    /* Forest plot display */
proc sgplot data=master noautolegend;
title 'Forest Plot for Overall Survival (OS) - Subgroup Analysis';
    /* HR Plot */
scatter y=col0 x=HazardRatio /
xerrorupper=HRUpperCL
xerrorlower=HRLowerCL
markerattrs=(symbol=circlefilled);
    /* Display columns on x2 axis */
scatter y=col0 x=col11 / markerchar=col1 x2axis;
scatter y=col0 x=col12 / markerchar=col2 x2axis;
scatter y=col0 x=col13 / markerchar=col3 x2axis;
    refline 1 / axis=x;
refline 1 / axis=x lineattrs=(pattern=shortdash) transparency=0.5;
    xaxis offsetmin=0 offsetmax=0.70 min=0 max=2 minor display=(nolabel);
x2axis offsetmin=0.4 display=(noticks nolabel);
yaxis display=(noticks nolabel) offsetmin=0.1 offsetmax=0.05;
    footnote 'Hazard Ratio is based on Cox Regression (placebo as reference group), with <1 favoring treatment';
run;
```

Conclusion

Effective collaboration between statisticians and statistical programmers is essential in conducting robust statistical analyses, developing specifications for analysis datasets, and generating accurate analytical results. For statistical programmers working in oncology, a solid understanding of survival analysis, therapeutic guidelines, tumor response criteria (such as RECIST), and specific censoring or confirmation rules is crucial. This knowledge enhances their ability to interpret statistical analysis plans (SAPs) and mock shells accurately. Consequently, programmers can efficiently transform raw oncology data into meaningful analysis datasets and ensure the accurate creation and validation of outputs.

End Matter

About the Author

Shivaravindra is a seasoned Clinical SAS Programmer with deep expertise in oncology clinical trials. With a strong foundation in ADaM dataset development, survival analysis, and regulatory reporting, he has contributed to numerous successful submissions and complex analyses. As an educator and mentor, Shivaravindra is passionate about making clinical programming concepts easy to understand and practically applicable.

He is the creator of the popular YouTube channel Advanced SAS Interview Topics, which offers in-depth tutorials, mock interviews, and end-to-end project walkthroughs for aspiring and experienced SAS programmers.

? YouTube: Advanced SAS Interview Topics

Further Reading & Resources

CDISC ADaM and SDTM Implementation Guides

RECIST 1.1 Guidelines

FDA Guidance for Industry: Clinical Trial Endpoints for the Approval of Cancer Drugs and Biologics

Kaplan-Meier and Cox Proportional Hazards Model Documentation (SAS Institute)

Statistical Analysis Plan (SAP) and Mock Shells Best Practices